Whiskey Bent
and
Hell Bound

No Holiday for Justice

Bob McGregor

authorHOUSE®

AuthorHouse™
1663 Liberty Drive
Bloomington, IN 47403
www.authorhouse.com
Phone: 1-800-839-8640

First published by AuthorHouse 11/20/2009

ISBN: 978-1-4490-5145-7 (e)
ISBN: 978-1-4490-5143-3 (sc)
ISBN: 978-1-4490-5144-0 (hc)

Library of Congress Control Number: 2009912188

Printed in the United States of America
Bloomington, Indiana

This book is printed on acid-free paper.

Dedication
To Molly, John and Patrick

GUNSLINGERS AND WORDSMITHS

"THIS IS THE WEST. When the legend becomes fact, print the legend." The jaded editor of the Shinbone *Star* gave this advice to his enterprising young reporter who was about to write a story destroying the myth of *The Man Who Shot Liberty Valance*. This timeless movie, produced by John Ford, the classic director of Western movies, featured Jimmy Stewart, John Wayne and Lee Marvin. It remains one of Hollywood's better attempts at capturing the flavor of sagebrush on celluloid. The advice of the editor to his pup reporter added marrow to the bones of the collective mythology of the West. Wild Bill Hickok, Wyatt Earp, John Wesley Hardin, saloons filled with dance hall girls, hard-drinking and harder-living cowboys – all are part of the fabric of an American frontier based in truth, but steeped in legend.

Perhaps the most vivid image of that legend is a mental portrait of men settling their differences at high noon in the middle of a dusty street with six-guns. Largely apocryphal, the Main Street "high noon" face-off between gunslingers is an image reinforced by countless Hollywood oat burners. Throngs of red-blooded Americans over the span of decades continue to believe the myth of the "Wild West" to be an accurate portrayal of the "real" West. The collective psyche of several generations, both here and across Atlantic and Pacific, has been shaped significantly by Hollywood. Roy Rogers, Gene Autry and John Wayne more than exemplified the concept of "hands across the sea." Their "hands" had a stranglehold on the popular cultures of most of the civilized world. That grip was just as strong in London and Tokyo as it was in Omaha and Duluth.

The reality is that most people killed by gunfighters in the Old West were shot from ambush or gunned down in what rarely was a "fair" fight. The winner usually was the best back shooter in the bunch. He became the most feared of the gunslingers, at least until somebody who was meaner and sneakier came skulking into town with gun in hand. The honor and ethic of a fair fight were as grossly exaggerated then as now.

An updated version of the Western gunslinger is that of the courtroom shootist. We cling to the memory of Jimmy Stewart and George C. Scott squaring off in *Anatomy of a Murder*, or of Tom Cruise finding the courage, testosterone and a well-written script to challenge Jack Nicholson, the "take no prisoners" Marine Colonel in the witness chair in *A Few Good Men*. But simply because the legend may stretch the truth, the *vignettes* of Western lore normally were not woven from whole cloth. Similarly, these courtroom tales of dueling advocates, shooting at each other with their words and their wits, usually were very close to being the real McCoy and not the product of some imaginative screen writer's fertile and creative mind.

Just as with the gunslingers of the Old West, the courtroom legend of the word slinging advocate often surpasses the reality – but not always. Sometimes, the actual event is as good as advertised and is recounted for years afterward in the halls of justice and the coffee rooms of the court officials – be they judges, bailiffs, prosecutors, defense attorneys or court reporters, among others. All of these courthouse rats are trying to cadge a nibble from the same wheel of hoop cheese, the glory of having been there when the big shootout was waged.

We like to believe that good trial lawyers can be equated with the *pistoleros* of Laredo, Tucson and Dodge City. We admire and are thrilled by the epic drama played out in courthouses across the judicial frontiers of our country by the hired guns of the defense bar and their eternal adversaries, the state and federal prosecutors who work for the "guv'mint," as we say in the South.

We revel at the sound of their "slapping leather," even though their weapons of choice are their guile, their guts, their wits and their words. These tools of their trade can inflict psychological wounds every bit as grievous as the physical ones inflicted by the Colt .45, the preferred instrument of the deadliest of the Western gunslingers. But at least in a courtroom the adversaries collect a fee or draw a salary, and often have a few shots of Jack Daniels together at trial's end.

And yet, there really *is* something to the notion of the *mano a mano* face offs in today's courtrooms. Those face-offs, at their best, come closer than anything else we've got going to recreating the legend of the Dodge City gunfighter. Picture Robert Duvall's famous scene as the Air Cavalry Commander in *Apocalypse Now*: "I love the smell of napalm in the morning." ... "It smells like VICTORY!"

That one scene better characterizes what it feels like to be a genuine twenty-four- carat, meet you at high noon with iron on your hip, ass-kickin' *trial lawyer* than any course I ever took or lecture I ever heard. It certainly illustrates the quest for the blue ribbon or the gold medal in a courtroom face-off better than any bloodless and sissified "bureaucratese" ever uttered by a boss or supervisor spouting about "the skills of a successful advocate," or some similar drivel.

The pages of this book are filled with accounts of the prosecution, and often the preceding investigation, of assorted drug dealers, robbers, murderers, child molesters and other scions of our society that I met and prosecuted during my career. The bad men and blood-spilling thugs became a part of my life for more than twenty years. A few of the very worst of them are permanently embedded in my psyche, much to its detriment. I developed more than a passing relationship with the courtroom fast-draw artists of the defense bar who represented the bad guys, sometimes with a thinly disguised contempt for the human detritus that they represented, sometimes with a genuine passion for the "cause," but always with the desire to kick some prosecutor's ass.

The reader will also witness some of what really goes on in court-rooms across the country every day. Readers will feel the frustration of the victims who come seeking simple redress for the grievance inflicted on them by some bad guy, but frequently find eternally more grievance and frustration heaped upon them by a system that doesn't seem to care – and too often doesn't – than from the criminal himself. More than a few of the characters and situations in these pages are so strange as to almost defy belief, except to those who come to court on a daily basis and see for themselves this black comedy that we refer to as "justice."

I have included the accounts of a few miscreants prosecuted by a select group of men and women who wore that white hat and rode that white stallion, gripping the matched ivory handled pistols that they fired for justice. You'll come to know and admire these men and women who were the *top guns* of the prosecution. I came to see them as they really were – not comic-book heroes or mean-spirited automatons – just ordinary human beings with their own flaws and shortcomings, doing heroic work in the arena of justice. This book is my own attempt to make legend become reality. You'll also be introduced to some of the *black hats*, otherwise known as defense attorneys, with whom we prosecutors matched wits and guts on a daily basis. Proceed at your own risk!

My Days as a Gun Slinging Wordsmith

I worked as a state prosecutor, deputy district attorney (DDA), in Alabama in three judicial circuits for about eight years. And for slightly more than fourteen years I was an Assistant United States Attorney in the Northern District of Alabama. During my tenure in the legal arena of the courtroom and in the much larger "circus" of justice, I encountered defendants who ranged from stand-up bad guys who would just as soon tell a judge or a prosecutor to go straight to hell without passing "go," to totally depraved individuals who gave the rest of the criminal element a worse name than what they actually deserved. I encountered a few poor souls who had run afoul of the law, but who were otherwise likeable losers, usually while trying to be dead solid serious.

I also made the acquaintanceship or genuine friendship of numerous men and women in the criminal defense bar. The overwhelming majority of these defenders of the accused were very hard-working, highly professional members of the Bar who had the very difficult job of mounting the best defense available to them, and within the strictures of ethics afforded by our profession. In fact, the Alabama Rules of Professional Responsibility is older than any written code of ethics extant in any other state in the Union. Nonetheless, we all went at each other hammer and tong in the courtroom. At trial's end, verdict not withstanding, we'd shake hands, and likely as not have a drink with each other when the shoutin' and shootin' was over and done. And that's the part about being a lawyer most people just don't understand. But, as they say, it comes with the territory.

As a DDA I prosecuted cases in three separate and distinct judicial circuits. These three jurisdictions were comprised of a total of five counties varying in size and cultural differences roughly akin to the distinctions between plow horses and thoroughbreds. The counties ranged from rural and sparsely populated Shelby, Coosa and Clay counties, to big, bad-ass, and mostly urban, Mobile and Jefferson counties, home to the two most populous cities in the state, Mobile and Birmingham.

During the time that I was a "fed" in the Northern District of Alabama, my jurisdiction consisted of thirty-one counties, an area which encompassed roughly the northern third of the state with the main office being located in Birmingham. Also, I was specially authorized by the Justice Department to investigate and prosecute federal cases in the Northern District of Georgia, and to coordinate investigations – with both state and federal agencies involved – in those two jurisdictions, as well as that of the Eastern District of Tennessee. Over the course of my career, I became a familiar figure in several courthouses and with more than a few law enforcement agencies throughout the tri-state area.

And I loved every minute of doing for pay what I gladly would have done for free. Okay, I exaggerate slightly about the remuneration, but it's close to the truth. Chasing bad guys and putting them in prison was about as much fun as anything I could do with my clothes on. For several years I had a sign displayed on the outside of my office door that accurately described my attitude toward my job: *If I'm at work, somebody's goin' to jail!*

I also had a brass sign, about eight inches by three inches, situated prominently on my desk, and which my wife had purchased years before at a yard sale. I don't know how the party selling it came to possess it, unless some Catholic Church had unloaded it in a going-out-of-business sale. But the sign was perfect for my purposes. It read: "Confessions 5:00 to 7:00 Daily."

I got my kicks from writing search warrant affidavits, accompanying cops and agents to crime scenes and interrogating suspects. Above all, I would pay a handsome sum for the privilege of selecting a jury and trying a good case with some genuine bad guys as defendants. I've never been an addict of any kind, but I imagine that a hard-core crack head doesn't get the wallop from sucking on his pipe that I got from delivering a closing argument to twelve good and true citizens.

The very best prosecutors have a fire burning in the belly that is fed by the fuel of pride, ego and the will to see justice done. Those select few, of which I was occasionally designated, had both the fire and the cool detachment necessary to rise to the top. I had the fire, but only rarely the cool detachment. I was like a shooting star – brilliant for brief periods of time – but lacking in the endurance and iron will necessary to generate sufficient thought from my mind to control the passion from my heart. But I was light on my feet, and usually could summon from memory sufficient statutory references and relevant precedents when arguing a legal principle in the courtroom. In short, the soul of the Irish poet in me blended rather nicely with my fighting Scotsman's occasional lust for blood, all unsullied by an over abundance of scholarship, vital to an appellate lawyer, only a means to an end to a "courtroom" lawyer.

Much to my displeasure, there was a sea change in Justice Department policies, which occurred sometime in the mid to late 1990s. Those policies altered our daily routine to the point that administrative requirements began to eclipse prosecutorial duties. Supervisors became absolute sticklers for making everyone rigidly adhere to the Department's image of the perfect prosecutor – computer literate, skilled in the art of doing what secretaries once did, such as typing and taking dictation, never being late with worksheets or trial memoranda, and slavishly devoted to the principle of doing everything in accord with "the book."

Needless to say, the "trial dogs" in the office felt overburdened and under appreciated by management. These changes resulted in the stifling of creativity that separates the plow horses from the thoroughbreds in the courtroom. A once-proud group of ass-kicking courtroom warriors were gradually converted into a pack of visor-wearing, pencil-pushing bureaucrats. We became consumed with shuffling paper instead of putting bad guys in the federal joint where they belonged.

Those changes – and inventing imaginative ways of sticking it to anyone who had the temerity to fight City Hall – became the norm. Matt Hart, one of my colleagues, in a moment of profound insight which he experienced one night while filling out his daily, weekly and monthly forms, said it best: "Never let it be said that the United States Attorneys Office allowed the success of the mission to interfere with administrative correctness."

Too many top-of-the-line prosecutors became little more than numbers crunchers and official form generators. Too many forgot the thrill generated by the sight and smell of the freshly spilled blood of a defendant's attorney in a trial where the stakes were high – *Big Casino*. This conversion wasn't the fault of any one person or policy. It merely was the inevitable metamorphosis that infects virtually every organization, public or private, but particularly government agencies when a critical mass peculiar to that organization is achieved. But, I knew that my time was rapidly coming to an end. Ultimately, a variety of physical maladies forced me to take a disability retirement.

And so, I sit here and write about how it was "back in the day."

I was egotistical enough to think that I was irreplaceable; I wasn't. I overstayed my leave by stepping on toes, breaking rules and generally thumbing my nose at the office power structure. I learned that when you leave the employ of Uncle Sam, a phenomenon occurs that is similar to that of removing your foot from a bucket filled with water. You don't leave a hole in the water. It doesn't exist and never did – and neither did you.

But you still have your memories of being "on the job." Unfortunately, memories and the dime store trinkets that the Justice Department gave to you every five years for service are about all that you have after taking your final leave from what you had loved once, and now were leaving after being jilted by that same mistress. I felt pretty much the same way I felt after watching Tommy Kirk shoot the canine star of *Old Yeller*, his very own pooch that he loved as much as all of us loved our doggies when we too were young and innocent.

I was no virgin to the ways and practices of the federal bureaucracy when I first walked in the door. But it took me more than a decade to realize that I was not immune from being pulled under the waves that I generated by the tentacles of the giant squid of the bureaucracy. Foolishly, I believed that making big cases and then winning those in court somehow excused me from the more mundane requirements of the job. My mistaken estimation of my value to the leviathan that was the Justice Department resulted in my being fairly miserable for the last five or six years on the job.

Fourteen and a half years after taking the oath of allegiance to the United States, my status had changed from being the blushing bride who had lost her innocence - but only to the man she was marrying - to that of an aging and haggard hooker, just hoping that she could attract enough paying customers to put food in the mouths of her kids. I felt a real emptiness that would remain with me for many months. I turned in my key card, my "fed creds," and my laminated, 100 per cent- in-living color, hang-it-around-the neck with a federally-issued-lanyard, identification card.

I walked out the door for the last time, and I left the building. When that door slammed shut behind me, I became a member in good standing of the **K-MAG-YO-YO** club – **Kiss My Ass Goodbye; You're On Your Own!**

I had found out the hard way what a long-time colleague told me my first week on the job. He advised me that the federal government would treat me like an army mule: "First, they'll pile as much of a load on you as you can carry, and they'll keep on piling until they break your back. Then they'll shoot you. And then they'll eat you." He was right. I was cocky and thought that I could beat the system. I couldn't. Sooner or later, the "system" consumes everything and everyone it touches. I also learned, in one very specific instance, that even though you might win the battle, you almost guarantee that you will lose the war when you are hard-headed enough to take on the office power structure.

But when you get right down to it, the ultimate reason that I left a job that I loved, was that I was too sick to continue working. I had refused to acknowledge that I just wasn't physically capable any more of doing the job. Not that I was free from sin in the slightest. I have outlined a few of my inadequacies as an employee of the Justice Department, as opposed to doing my job the best way that I saw fit to accomplish the job of indicting and convicting bad guys, as well as actively working with my agents to ensure that the case that we put together gave us the best possible shot at making a case that would stick. And if that meant not having my "prosecutive memoranda" ready for inspection by my supervisors at the designated hour and minute, then so be it. I was never unprepared in court and had a reputation for trying cases that some prosecutors wouldn't touch because they thought the case couldn't be won, and I would win them.

The insights into the human species that I gained as a prosecutor, as well as the fading memories of my career now resided in the rearview mirror of my life's work, and were but a fading reflection of what once had been my life's very *raison de'tre*. I looked in that mirror and saw a bent, but not broken, old pug that still could not make himself get out of the ring, even though the arena was vacant and no one was listening, save the roustabouts who cleaned the floor after the animals had been returned to their cages.

During the more than two decades that I was a prosecutor, I learned more about the nature of good and evil than I ever wanted to know. Now, I can't forget those lessons even when I need to forget. I became more than casually familiar with the business, political and legal institutions of our society which, while morally neutral, assumed a mantle of an organic and almost spiritual quality reflective of the souls of the people who built them. Crediting some of them with even having souls is an exercise in pure hyperbole if not outright prevarication. I learned that the people pulling the strings in these institutions often were not the benign puppet masters of Punch and Judy. Some of them could have taught Machiavelli or Vito Corleone lessons in "making offers that can't be refused."

But, and perhaps the most important lesson that I learned in combating the evil doers and fighting to make them pay for their evil deeds, was a lesson that is etched in granite in the mind of every prosecutor worth his battle ribbons: Justice never takes a holiday! I learned that lesson by working holidays, weekends and late hours during the work week. And the reason for working those late hours when getting the job done required it, was the corollary to that last lesson that I learned. If justice never takes a holiday, it is only because crime and evil never take a holiday.

And, because of that eternal struggle between good and evil, every prosecutor who is serious about his job as well as the enormous responsibility that comes with it, should never forget the admonition of Bill Jordan, the old gunfighter, United States Marine and US Border Patrol agent: "In a gunfight, there is no second place winner." The same holds true in the courtroom: There is no second place winner.

My experiences and observations at times caused me to laugh, sometimes to cry, but always left me feeling more alive than I have ever felt, before or since. I shared feelings of a most personal nature with other prosecutors, cops and agents, even with more than a few criminal defense attorneys who had an understanding borne of experience as to what we do and who we are. It's the intersection of what *is*, with what we'd *like* it to be. I know that makes little sense to most people, but the brothers and sisters of our fraternity of justice get it.

I hope that this collection of my memories will give you at least a sliver of insight into that very tight-knit fraternity. And most of those memories have the added benefit of being true. At least in so far as any trial lawyer is capable of telling the truth. I came to realize during the organizing of my experiences in the courtroom that I couldn't begin to do justice to *all* of my memories as a prosecutor because of their sheer number.

Thus, this collection of selected courtroom ventures will be restricted to my experiences as a state prosecutor, and of those, just a slice. I will limit myself to sharing with you a few of the events, emotions and lessons I learned during my years as a deputy district attorney. I will attempt to tell you what I felt every time that I stood ramrod straight and announced to all assembled in the courtroom: "Ready for the State."

With that *caveat*, I say to you: This was my world. Welcome to it.

Chapter One

MY BIRTH AS A PROSECUTOR

WHEN THE BIG THIRTY rolled into my life, most of my contemporaries were all grown up and well into making their respective fortunes, having children and exhibiting many of the other signs of adulthood such as buying a house and joining Kiwanis. I was still treading water, looking for whatever niche in which I was proficient. One that made me want to jump out of bed every morning because I was so jazzed with whatever it was that would ring my chimes and stoke my fires.

I had tried my hand at several different jobs without having acquired anything of permanence, save a reasonably nice four-year old Mazda and very little debt. I discovered that my efforts to save the world by teaching history and civics to high school kids had, with a few gratifying exceptions, gone for naught because the world neither wanted nor needed saving. I had lots of fun and achieved a measure of fulfillment as a high school, college and club swimming coach, but did not have much in the way of material goods to show for my efforts. On the non-material acquisitions side of the ledger I made lifelong friendships and created some lasting memories. The experiences were worth it, but good times and good friends don't put money in your bank account, and they certainly don't pay the bills.

It was then that I scratched an old itch. In the fall of 1978 I entered the University of Alabama School of Law, my head filled with illusions of becoming a highly paid associate on the fast track to partner at a top shelf Birmingham firm. Either that or becoming a rich, famous, feared and admired reincarnation of Perry Mason while zealously and successfully defending the wrongfully accused. You know, just like real life.

Not being selected for either Law Review or Order of the Coif cured me of any aspirations that I had might ever have harbored of becoming a partner at the prestigious law firm of my musings. And with the dissolution of that pipe dream also went my vision of knocking down six figures, driving a silver Benz and living in a modest little dwelling house, worth perhaps $400 K, in one of the older, more traditional areas of Mountain Brook with my adoring wife and highly achieving children.

If I had, in fact, attained such a level of academic excellence as to merit a job with a *silk stocking*, high paying firm, I would have been miserable, as would the members of the firm who hired me, ability notwithstanding. And I wouldn't have been there long enough for the senior partners to even learn my name. Something about trying to dress up a pig in a tuxedo for a formal ball comes to mind. It just doesn't work.

I was born to chase fire engines, play cops and robbers and "preach," regardless of who wanted to hear what I had to say. Fortunately, I entered that area of the law that I was born to enter while being paid for my efforts – that of a career prosecutor. As well as allowing me to get my kicks from chasing those fire engines, which turned out to be police patrol cars, and helping the cops to catch the robbers, every time I took a case to trial I had a captive audience of twelve citizens. They at least had to pretend to listen to me, or the judge would send her bailiff to wake up the offender. Glorious!

My experiences as an intern with the Shelby County District Attorney's Office prior to my third year in law school erased all illusions I might once have had about the plight of the "wrongfully accused"– an egregious oxymoron rivaled only by "military intelligence." I was an unpaid flunky, otherwise known as a law clerk, and I got credit for my "clerkship" in the fall semester of my third year of law school for working at that office during the summer preceding my senior year. I was issued a third year practice card that summer after my second year, a privilege which the Alabama Supreme Court afforded to me and others similarly situated.

With the permission of the court and opposing counsel, and with the presence of a licensed attorney from my office, I was entrusted to run wild with whatever motions, preliminary hearings and misdemeanors needed arguing or trying. I loved it and was as happy as a bear cub chasing butterflies every time that I got to act like a lawyer. My working there that summer resulted in my being offered a "real" job with that office, contingent on my graduating and passing the bar examination. Fortunately for me and my wife, I managed to clear both those hurdles.

COLUMBIANA – MAYBERRY REDUX, *OR* THE REIGN OF THE COURTHOUSE IRREGULARS

AFTER GRADUATING FROM LAW school in the late spring of 1981, I passed the bar examination in July, though I did not receive the written notice of my acceptance as a member of the State Bar of Alabama until the first week of October. I then began my journey as a deputy district attorney in the Eighteenth Judicial Circuit – Shelby, Coosa and Clay Counties. I was traveling down the *highway to jus-*

tice, or the *road to perdition*, as some of my friends who represent the *dark side* (criminal defense attorneys), often refer to the path taken by prosecutors. We prosecutors know that path by its proper names, the *Glory Road* or the *Stairway to Heaven.*

I picked up where I had left off as an intern the previous summer of 1980. Shelby was the most populous of the three counties in the Circuit. The main office was in Columbiana, County Seat of Shelby, and it was where the District Attorney, Billy Hill, and all of his assistants drank coffee, talked politics and occasionally went to court. Sometimes, we even tried a case when we couldn't settle it or get it continued to the next trial docket.

When court was in session in Ashland, in Clay County; or Rockford in Coosa County; we prosecutors would saddle up and ride to these outposts on the frontier of our Circuit, ostensibly to bring justice to the citizenry. If the mountain wouldn't come to Mohammad, then Mohammad would go to the mountain. "Bringing justice" often consisted of being present for an arraignment docket at the courthouse for about an hour, followed by a two-hour lunch at the local greasy spoon, sometimes with the High Sheriff and on occasion, with one of the several judges, district or circuit, as our luncheon companions.

And for the edification and continuing education of you Carpetbaggers, we of the Southern persuasion really do eat fried green tomatoes. Throw in some fried chicken or hamburger steak with onions and gravy laid on thick, along with two other vegetables, cornbread and sweet tea, and you had yourself some good eatin' for about $3.50 plus the tip. Add seventy-five cents for the banana pudding, and you would still walk out with enough change in your pocket for a late afternoon "Co' Coler" back at the courthouse before waddling out to the car and heading home for a nice dinner. Need you *really* ask why too many prosecutors are fat? Excepting, of course, the ones in California who spend half a day with their personal trainer at Gold's Gym and the other half gorging themselves with something really exotic like alfalfa sprouts smothered in low-cal rutabaga salad dressing.

On those rare occasions, however, when there was a case that *had* to be tried, we'd earn our pay. A few of those would be as bloody and evil as any crime committed in three episodes of Law and Order. The hinterlands of Alabama can't touch Atlanta, New Orleans or Birmingham in the number or rate of crimes committed, but the ones that stand out for their sheer wickedness and brutality match up with those committed in the South Bronx any day of any week.

But most of the crimes and "misunderstandings" that we handled in the rural Eighteenth Judicial Circuit were those that you might expect Barney Fife and Sheriff Andy to dispatch with some country wisdom and a stern lecture. It was during that summer of 1980 that I spent working as an unpaid intern when I first became acquainted with the members of the "tribe," or the "courthouse irregulars" as I occasionally referred to them. I would become even more familiar with them and their ways once I began work as a "for real" prosecutor in the fall of 1981. Every courthouse has folks with nothing better to do than, well, hang around the courthouse. Shelby Count just had more than its share. And they all seemed to be from another planet "Seemed?" Hell! They *were* from another planet.

But they were harmless, and could be quite amusing on most occasions. On other occasions, they could be a real pain in the ass, and I'm not talking about that damned government mule that I later learned was me. One or more of the irregulars would appear from time to time, usually with a grievance of some sort, be it real or imagined. The grievance, dispute, tort, crime, or whatever combination of legal wrongs that constituted these disputes, normally would be with one or more of the other tribe members. My job was to dissuade them from using the court system as their own private instrument of vengeance. I continued to intervene in their internecine squabbles for my entire tenure in that office.

If nothing else, the irregulars shared certain traits that usually would leave our office with evidence of their visits – sometimes for days afterwards. Early on in my clerkship, I noticed a large, economy-sized container of Lysol spray disinfectant and deodorant displayed on a table within a few feet of the front door to the office. Naively, I asked Bob Williams, the Chief Deputy, why we didn't store the can in the closet with the other cleaning supplies. He smiled and said "You'll find out." And I did – in spades. The first time that one of the irregulars made her presence known to our receptionist, I learned why the spray can of Lysol was within easy reach of our front-office personnel. I smelled Emma Lane before I heard or saw her. That same sickening aroma, redolent of dead fish and high-test B.O. also served as a calling card for the remaining members of the tribe.

My initial reaction to the noxious odor, which seemed to be a genetic imprint of each member of the tribe like a birthmark or an extra finger, was to maintain a facade of civility, and to refrain from engaging in a wide-spread fumigation counter-strike. My gentlemanly Southern upbringing survived only my initial meeting with Miss Emma. On subsequent visits, she didn't even seem to notice my obvious olfactory discomfort or my blatantly open attempts to quickly inoculate myself as well as the reception area with the spray deodorant.

Apparently without taking offense, she nonchalantly obeyed my command to stand by the door while I sprayed the vestibule with the perfumed aerosol. The most charitable thing that I can say about

Miss Emma's appearance and fragrance is that she might best be described as the antidote to Viagra. Not so charitably, but absolutely accurately, her looks were such that she could knock a starvin' wolf off a meat wagon. She looked sixty-five, but probably wasn't a day more than forty-five. All of these attributes obviously were the product of modern eugenics. The outer layer of dirt on her body was caked so thick, she probably had to use a spatula to scrape it off at Christmas and Easter. And she couldn't have had more than half a dozen teeth, both real and store-bought, in her mouth at any given time. But what she lacked in looks, she more than made up for with wit, personality and the charm of a fifth-generation debutante from Mobile or Montgomery.

Miss Emma would drop by from time to time either to register a complaint about one of the other members of the tribe, or to share with us the condition of her back, which she claimed to have injured while engaged in mortal combat with another member of the tribe, usually ten-year old Claude Ingram, Jr. Her chosen method of "telling" anyone about her back was to employ her normal salutation of "Hey, man," while immediately following up with an invitation to inspect the locus of her invisible injury. She would turn her back, and before you could run or shoot, would bend over at the waist, raise her dress and invite you to inspect her "injury." I can assure you that the image of Emma Lane displaying her backside would scare dogs and traumatize small children. We in the D.A.'s Office, being the tough professional crime fighters –courtroom warriors – that the mean streets of Columbiana had made us, merely remained stoic before throwing up.

As an illustration of the tribe's notion of having a good time, and also perhaps of its breeding habits, I need only to relate to you the last time that I recall Miss Emma coming to the office. She was seeking legal redress against her intermittent nemesis and partner in mischief, Claude Ingram, Jr., the previously referenced juvenile, who either was the future of the tribe or its last hurrah. On this occasion, which proved to be her swan song to me prior to my exodus to Mobile County, she came seeking a warrant against the young miscreant.

Foolishly, but driven by my curiosity as well as my desire to play the role of the helpful public servant, I asked the Empress of the Egg and Butter Road (No kidding; you can find it on any map of Shelby County.) what the little delinquent had done to merit being the target of an arrest warrant. She responded that he had been "messin'" with her dog. I told her that tormenting her dog in some vague fashion probably didn't constitute a crime, and that she should simply tell Claude to go home. Once again, she was talking apples, and I was hearing oranges. I still wasn't fully versed in the life style and habits of the tribe. Miss Emma then set me straight: "No man, I mean he's been "*messin'*" with my dog."

A truly terrible image slowly but ever so surely formed in my subconscious and crystallized as it moved into the area of my brain that was a repository for fully conscious thoughts. I began to understand what was taking place between Claude Ingram and Miss Emma's dog and it wasn't a pretty picture. I hastily suggested that she throw a bucket of cold water on the two of them and forget about prosecution. I then showed her the door, sprayed the reception area with the Lysol once again, and knew that I needed either a change of venue or a very long vacation. Claude had succeeded in giving the otherwise beautiful concept of "puppy love" a really ugly meaning. But who was I to judge? I had begun to think that the entire world was populated with the likes of the tribe. There still are days when what is left of my mind embraces that same conclusion.

A final footnote to the hard life and fast times of Miss Emma Lane is that, notwithstanding the fact that any attempts she made to improve her looks and personal hygiene were tantamount to attempting to turn a sow's ear into a silk purse, on occasion she made the effort to keep up with the fashion of the times. When a strikingly attractive young California beauty named Bo Derek introduced white women in America to cornrows in the movie *Ten*, well, you guessed it, sport! Miss Emma's next trip to the courthouse marked her Bo Derek phase. Although she failed miserably in her attempts to become the first, and perhaps only, Caucasian resident of Columbiana to braid cornrows from her less than golden hair, you really had to admire her unflagging optimism and efforts at self improvement.

For the sake of history and posterity I must continue with the cast of characters. Their antics and memories are as worthy of preservation as those of any other primitive society. Margaret Mead would have been in anthropologist's heaven had she graced Columbiana with her presence in the heyday of "the tribe." Soon, these denizens of that hamlet will be but wisps of smoke, forgotten by all but those of us who were there. General McArthur and Frankie Patterson were two more unforgettable members of the courthouse irregulars. Both sported, though not necessarily simultaneously, World War I style leather flying caps of the kind worn by Snoopy when he was chasing the Red Baron. And they wore them indoors and out, regardless of season or weather. I never did figure out whether the pair of them shared one cap in the communal spirit they often exhibited, or whether each had his own. It doesn't really matter. My curiosity about such meaningless matters merely demonstrates the truth of the old maxim that "idle hands are the devil's workshop."

And those two, unfortunately for them, but more so for the gene pool, were the product of some unholy workshop where a less-than-benevolent fallen angel amused himself with his "creations." They were living, breathing evidence - virtual icons of Darwinian thought - that man evolved from lower life forms, a still hotly disputed theory, at least in Shelby County. John Scopes would have felt redeemed had he known Frankie and the General.

Frankie Patterson always walked around with a near toothless grin plastered across his otherwise-beyond-salvation face. And when a Frankie Patterson grin is your strong suit, you know that an orangutan may feel an entirely unnatural attraction toward you. Truth be told, the attraction likely will be mutual. Frankie wasn't a bad guy, just dumb as a sack of hammers, and not much to look at unless you really liked orangutans. He did, however, manage to accumulate quite a criminal history consisting mainly of alcohol-related offenses and minor assaults against one or another member of the tribe. These transgressions often resulted in Frankie's arrest with his judgment day being marked on the misdemeanor docket of district judge, now Alabama Supreme Court Justice, Patti Smith. He would always draw a stern warning and sometimes a brief jail sentence from the good judge.

Judge Patti was one of those rare and special people within the judicial system, an excellent jurist, a delightful person and somebody who was actually in the game to help people, as well as to mete out the appropriate measure of justice. Not to mention the undisputed fact that she was the best looking judge in at least the entire Southeast. Blond hair, blue eyes and a smile known to make the knees of strong men weak with stupidity, were just a few of her more outstanding traits. And, if anything, she had a personality and smarts to match her judicial presence. Her husband Jerry should thank the dear Lord on a daily basis for blessing him with such an angel.

Judge Patti, no bleeding heart of the sort who would make prosecutors grind their teeth with frustration at seeing probation handed out like judicial lollipops to genuine bad dudes, would, if the situation required it, put you in the cooler so fast that you might suffer frostbite. However, if you weren't really bad, just so ignorant that you were likely to be rejected as a guest on the Jerry Springer Show, stupidly stubborn or more in need of help than incarceration, Judge Patti would go the extra mile for you. But once she had gone that mile for you, you crossed her at your own peril.

And she saw Frankie Patterson appear before her bench with disturbing regularity. And when Frankie wasn't on Judge Patti's docket, his name often could be found on the docket of one of the local municipal court judges.' There wasn't much to be gained by putting Frankie in the slammer for more than two or three days. It didn't bother him in the slightest, and he occupied more space than he was worth.

Come to think of it, Frankie was Columbiana's version of Otis of Mayberry. Judge Patti or one of those municipal judges, often would sentence Frankie to serve a few days in the cooler, mainly to let him sober up, but also to maintain the fiction that going to jail was the panacea for solving our insoluble problems – poverty, illegitimacy, and the disappearance of something we used to call a conscience.

Years after I left Shelby County, either the Birmingham *News* or the Birmingham *Post Herald*, ran a lengthy series on multiply convicted drunk drivers in Alabama. The article highlighted what reasonably could be termed "Alabama's Drunk Drivers Hall Of Fame". My old buddy Frankie Patterson was the salutatorian of this class of motorized lushes. I feel certain that he would have won valedictory honors but for the fact that *numero uno* on the list, being several years older than Frankie, had a pretty good head start on him. Absent that handicap, I am positive that Frankie would have captured the pole position. His drunken driving citations ran the gamut from urban to rural venues, night or day violations, with varying degrees of intoxication ranging from pleasantly high to clinically dead.

Thank God that he apparently managed to keep whatever he was driving in the road, and never killed anyone. I guess that on occasion the Lord really does protect drunks and fools. Since that time however, the law has changed such that conviction of more than one driving under the influence offense within a certain period of time is a felony offense with at least some mandatory period of incarceration. But when Frankie was racking up his truly magnificent record of convictions, DUI was always a misdemeanor regardless of whether it was your first or fiftieth conviction.

GUNNY SACKS, POSSUMS AND GENERAL MCARTHUR

GENERAL MCARTHUR, *AKA* THE General, visited our office from time to time, usually complaining of some transgression, or simply to entertain anyone within hearing range with tales of his bravado in the Second World War. His most amazing feat, which he loved to recount in vivid detail, was his rescue of President Roosevelt's daughter during the Second World War. And you thought that FDR didn't even have a daughter.

According to the General, he made his body serve as an extension of a railroad track that had been sabotaged by Nazi spies, thus preventing a fatal wreck of the train that was transporting the First Daughter. In case you're wondering, the movie *Superman*, which had a similar scene involving Lois Lane, was being shown in local theaters about this time in Montevallo, closest city to Columbiana with a "pitcher show." Regardless, I'm sure that the original McArthur and Roosevelt would have been honored.

But the most vivid memory I have of the General is of observing him in the reception area one day chatting with an obviously nervous secretary – receptionist. She was staring at a gunny sack which he was holding in one hand by the neck, and which apparently contained…God knows what, because the sack was twisting and squirming in his hand as he made one-way small talk with the receptionist. I decided that a casual inquiry was the best approach, and so I asked him what the sack contained. I still wish that I had fetched our Chief Deputy and let him handle the matter. I might have had the privilege of observing the smooth-talking office ramrod go head to head with the General and come out on the short end of the gunny sack.

As it turned out, I handled the situation myself and ended up feeling like a cross between Marlin Perkins of the old *Zoo Parade* television show and Frank Buck of *Bring 'Em Back Alive* fame. Once I got the General's attention, I posed the $64 question, making relatively polite inquiry as to the contents of the sack. He just looked at me slyly and asked whether I wanted to see his 'possum. It could have been worse; at least the critter was alive. I politely declined his invitation and directed him to return with his 'possum to whatever dimension from whence they came. He complied, and the next time that I saw him, he was lacking both the gunny sack as well as the 'possum. But I can assure you that I maintained a healthy distance from him. For all that I knew he could have been toting a rattlesnake in his pocket.

We usually would see one or more members of the tribe when official court business was conducted every Wednesday for the purpose of handling the traffic docket, felony preliminary hearings, and misdemeanor court, which dealt with guilty pleas and the occasional trial. These proceedings were overcrowded, often confusing and intensive, not to mention tense. Thus was born the name and concept of, "Wacky Wednesday." Of course, many citizens other than members of the tribe were summoned to these weekly dramas, including police officers, deputy sheriffs and state troopers when there was a trial or preliminary hearing scheduled, as well as defendants, witnesses and the aggrieved victims.

No more than half the defendants would come to court with attorneys. When they did, I dealt with the attorney. When a defendant would show up *pro se*, or on behalf of himself, I normally would play the role of both prosecutor as well as defense attorney. Well, didn't that present me with a conflict of interest? Of course it did. But, I soon discovered that most people would knowingly waive their right to be represented by counsel, and that most of them simply wished to tell their side of the dispute and would depend on me to be fair with them. Anytime that I saw a real legal problem looming, I would get the case continued and do my best to convince these lambs to return to court on the appointed date with a mouthpiece in tow.

Most of the misdemeanors, and some felony preliminary hearings, that we handled were minor assaults, petty thefts, checks that bounced for insufficient funds and boundary line disputes. The boundary line cases could prove to be fascinating in that most started out as trespassing cases, often escalated to assaults and sometimes blew up to shootouts where everybody got charged by John Law with attempted murder. The police most often copped the attitude that they would just arrest everybody and let God and the DA sort it out.

And even after a shootout which resulted in serious felony charges being brought against every weed in the garden, they would wind up being what they should have been in the first case – misdemeanor trespassing offenses. Judge Patti would have a group butt chewing in open court and then place the thoroughly chastened defendants on two years probation. And we normally wouldn't see any of them again for at least two years. Sometimes, seemingly complex and nearly insoluble problems have very simple solutions. I'll elaborate in the next few paragraphs more precisely what I mean by taking the complex problem and reducing it to the lowest common denominator with the simplest solution possible – all the while still achieving what passes for justice.

THE PRICE OF JUSTICE – OR THE FINE ART OF BEING A RUG MERCHANT

COMMON SENSE AND A little bit of experience will take a prosecutor a long way in recognizing the worth of a case in deciding whether and how to settle it. Settling a case – accepting a guilty verdict either to the offense charged or to something less than that, and making a recommendation to the judge as to the appropriate sentence, is essential to our judicial system. Cursed by the ignorant masses, "plea bargaining" – without which the entire system would come to a grinding halt – must be employed judiciously and must adhere to several basic principles. Failure to learn and to adhere to these principles has cost more than one prosecutor his job, and on occasion has cost his boss the next election.

You see, the big secret that nobody wants to talk about is that people charged with crimes could absolutely break down the entire criminal justice system simply by demanding their right to a trial. Thank God that as of yet, most of the mutts charged with criminal violations haven't figured out that merely by insisting that a jury judge their guilt or innocence as is guaranteed by the Constitution, they could wreak havoc in the judicial branch of our government.

Of course, the system wouldn't break unless there was a concerted effort by defendants working together to achieve their notion of the "common good". Not likely to happen since prosecutors – and most judges – would make the first few of those demanding a trial pay dearly upon their being convicted. And the notion of working for the common good would never fly with these defendants unless they could get a guarantee that they could be first in the judicial welfare line. Fat chance!

Of course, if they did pull such a rotten trick as to insist upon their rights being scrupulously observed and adhered to, ultimately the legislative and executive branches would become mired down with the spillover problems generated by those in the judiciary – problems such as prison overcrowding, serious infringement on a person's right to a speedy trial and so forth. However, should such chaos ever actually occur, I can assure you that ultimately, the general populace would revive and refine the time-honored principles of self help, (vigilantism) self-defense and payback in a way scarcely envisioned by the founders.

Thus, prosecutors dispose of the vast majority of criminal cases by providing most defendants an incentive of sorts to admit their wrongdoing and take their medicine like the good little felons that most of them were raised to be by Momma and Poppa. That incentive normally would be a recommended sentence by the prosecutor in exchange for a guilty plea to the offense charged or sometimes to a lesser offense than the one charged. Plea bargaining at the Shelby County Courthouse on Wacky Wednesdays was about as close to fairness as the judicial system gets.

There was more than one occasion when I felt like Monty Hall on *Let's Make a Deal*. But there was a rough sense of justice to it all, and it was the kind of justice that most ordinary folks – and no

college professors – understood. If you're bad, then you get punished. If you take or break something that isn't yours, you pay for it
or replace it. And if you shoot somebody that just needs killin,' you
might have to serve a year or two, unless the scoundrel *really* needed
killin.' Then the community might reward you with the key to the
city or even a nominal honorarium. However, even if the deceased
happened to be a prime candidate for a bullet, but also was related by
blood or marriage to the owner of a large local business which was
the major source of jobs in the area, the otherwise heroic defendant
might be the recipient of an honorarium he didn't knowingly seek
nor particularly want – a cell with "Bubba" or "Lee Roy" for an extended period of time at the state big house.

We didn't have too many college professors in Columbiana and
environs, just a lot of common folks with good common sense. By
employing this system of "plea bargaining," each side got a little of
what it wanted and a little of something it didn't want. But it lu-
bricated the wheels of justice, and they turned steadily and were not
locked into place by an overabundance of trials. And this system of
providing an incentive to "fess up," admit guilt and take the bargain-
basement price of "doin' the time for doin' the crime," works the same
way in New York City as it does, and did, in Columbiana, Alabama.

Obviously, there was a stick as well as a carrot built into the system. The other side of that coin was what is known as a "trial tax."
Go to trial, and if a guilty verdict is returned, the sentence imposed
by the judge most often reflected the reality that the defendant had
foolishly elected to stand on his rights in total disregard of the system. Well, that's not fair is it? But if it's fair you're looking for, go
shoot pool at the local emporium. Just don't shoot a rack with a
poor-mouthing stranger who carries his own cue. We deal in justice,
not fairness. If we were both good and lucky, sometimes the two

coincided. And if "ifs and buts were candy and nuts, we'd all have a happy Christmas."

Think of a discount store. Such mercantile institutions sell their products for less money than the same item would cost in a mom and pop operation down the street. Loyalty to the store's owners, a sense of security in the honesty of the owner and in the quality of the goods being sold, are about the only things that keep the mom and pop operation from going out of business when competing with the discount store. A jury trial is much the same as the mom and pop store; it's the great leveler and insures that the defendant at least will see that he has received due process.

And he might just get lucky and hear those magical words rarely heard by defendants: "Not Guilty." Of course, since he very likely *is* guilty, most of the time the reviewing body that we call a jury will return that verdict. And then he will be sentenced, very likely to more time than that offered by the prosecutor. Some defense attorneys, particularly early in their careers, will object to a defendant being "punished" for exercising his constitutional right to a trial. But remember, a plea *bargain* is just that – a bargain. It is tantamount to the price one pays at a discount store – less than the price offered at the mom and pop operation, mainly because of the far greater volume of business conducted at the discount store, just lacking in the personal touch.

Without question or exception, my most notable plea negotiation, bargain and satisfaction of same occurred sometime during that summer of 1980. The following events occurred on a Wacky Wednesday misdemeanor docket, and the day was hot, irritating and long. It seemed that every red necked imbecile in the county had a case of some sort set on that particular docket. Even Judge Patti, ordinarily a model of cheerfulness and restraint, seemed just a bit put off with the confusion and aggravation of dealing with all those citizens and their problems.

I had no help on that particular day from any other deputy district attorney and essentially was ram rodding the citizens through the chute of justice by myself, all the while keeping the paperwork accurate and current, breaking up logjams and widening bottlenecks in the day's parade. And certainly I was working as hard as possible to keep the judge happy by disposing of the mass of cases on the docket as expeditiously as possible.

BILLY, BUCKY AND THE BEAVER

I SUPPOSE THAT IT was fated that such a hectic session in court would include the strange case of Billy Graham and the beaver hunter, set for preliminary hearing or plea to a reduction in the charged offense from a felony to a misdemeanor. No, not *that* Billy Graham, but Billy Graham, Columbiana's entrepreneur deluxe, Jack of all trades, master of none, etc. Billy was known by one and all around Columbiana as one of the last of a breed of real men who were honest-to-God patriots, and who didn't want the oppressive yoke of government restricting their freedoms, except, of course, when they needed the government to serve their ends. And that particular Wednesday marked one of those occasions when Billy wanted the law to stand up for his rights.

The defendant, Graham believed, had destroyed a beaver dam which happened to be on Mr. Graham's property. The destruction was caused by a well-placed stick of dynamite. The aggrieved victim of this unlawful attack upon his property presented a fact scenario to me that at least was sufficient to justify the warrant clerk's having issued a warrant for the defendant's arrest on a felony charge involving the unlawful destruction of property of another whose value exceeded a certain amount of money. I wasn't even slightly familiar with how one assessed the fair market value of a beaver dam, but I was game to learn.

The name of the object of Billy's wrath, I mean the defendant's name, has long ago slipped from my fading memory, but I sure remember his profession. After introducing myself to the accused – of course he didn't have a lawyer – I made the mistake of asking him what he did for a living. He looked me square in the eye and responded: "I'm a professional beaver hunter". I couldn't help myself, and blurted out a response before adequate reflection. "Aren't we all, sir, aren't we all"? Fortunately, this witty, but somewhat naughty *bon mot* (Or is that *double entendre?*) was lost upon its intended audience, and Judge Patti was out of earshot. After more crafty questioning on my part, it struck me that the coot really *was* a professional beaver hunter and that he trapped the creatures and collected a state bounty for their pelts. Whoever said that capitalism and the frontier spirit had disappeared in this country? Not in Shelby County, Bucko!

Apparently, Alabama had a real pest problem with these woodsy critters. For all I knew, prior to my being in court that day and receiving a quick tutorial from the Great White Hunter, they did nothing more harmful than shill for Ipana toothpaste in my youth. Surely you remember Bucky Beaver of Saturday morning kid's T.V. fame, that flat-tailed little huckster with the bad overbite. But they also have a nasty habit of felling trees by gnawing them at the base and then using them for beaver housing, clubs, skateboards, what have you. Many property owners, however, wish to put them out of the lumber business – permanently. Thus, there was a state bounty for beaver pelts which created whatever need there was for the existence of professional beaver hunters like… I'll just call him "Bucky" since I can't recall his given name.

It took Bucky all of about fifteen minutes to give me a primer in beaver hunting, which ranged from his occasional employment of "beaver hounds" to track the "scutters," to his use of a "beaver hook" to snag the varmints if they tried to save their pelts from being converted to a two dollar check payable to bearer by the state of Alabama. Cruel? Perhaps, but Mother Nature can be an uncaring bitch when she grows weary of the tree huggers and granola eaters.

Besides learning from Bucky the finer points of the use of a beaver hook, I also managed to extract an admission from him that, yes, he had blown up Brother Billy's beaver dam with a stick of dynamite. His use of this weapon of mass destruction on the beaver dam was done in a singular moment of greed and laziness. And now, Mr. Graham came to court seeking justice, retribution and restitution. And, like most aggrieved victims anywhere in a chicken dropping sort of case, restitution would be just fine should justice and retribution prove difficult or impossible to obtain.

The fine art of negotiation is practiced in bazaars and flea markets all over the world, and it certainly has been honed to a fine point in courts of justice throughout this great country of ours. I didn't know much about how to succeed in this ancient art when I first began practicing law, but I have never been better at it than I was in court that day in Columbiana, county seat of Shelby, and home of the courthouse where justice sometimes was dispensed to the great unwashed masses.

Billy Graham informed me that his loss for the beaver dam and its dear departed critters would be approximately $2,000, give or take a few *dineros* : A bold opening bid on Billy's part. Perhaps he had me pegged as a wet behind the ears, bottom man on the totem pole Assistant D.A. who, in his zeal to protect the interests of the "people," would take the bait and run with it. This, of course, was a fairly accurate appraisal of me at that point in my career. But, looks can be deceiving, and even my lowly status and obvious inexperience did not mean that I was the complete fish that Billy had envisioned, hook set firmly in my mouth, ready to be filleted and fried.

And speaking of fish, that was the commodity that Billy claimed was worth the $2,000 restitution he was seeking. It seems that the pond created by the beaver dam was serving as the fishery for rainbow trout that Billy asserted he was cultivating for sale. At least that was Billy's story. Unfortunately for Mr. Graham, he could produce no corroboration for his claim – no receipts, no photographs of a prized fish or two, no witnesses to his prowess as a trout entrepreneur, not even the name of another fishery where he could have bought the fingerlings.

But, apparently, Billy was an adherent of the maxim that it doesn't hurt to ask. He just got greedy and asked for too much, a common failing of more than a few people seeking legal redress. Any monetary amount would have been too much for the somewhat less than egregious, and highly specious, "crime" committed by Bucky. But in the interests of settling the matter and leaving the aggrieved parties with their dignity, freedom and money somewhat intact, the three of us achieved *détente*. Following some furious back and forth negotiating between the two parties with my acting as referee and translator, we arrived at a plea agreement that I guarantee is unique in the annals of American jurisprudence beyond the boundaries of Shelby County.

And the look on Judge Patti's face when I stated the terms of the agreement was worth the price of admission. In fact, her initial response made me hasten to assure her that I wasn't playing games with the court: "Mr. McGregor, it is a hot day, and I am in no mood for fish *or* beaver stories". After hastily reassuring Her Honor that I was absolutely serious and would never play games with the court, I restated the terms of the agreement. "Bucky" would plead guilty to a reduced charge of misdemeanor criminal mischief. He would be sentenced to a term of six months in the county jail, suspended for two years pending his good behavior, which included not blowing up any more of Billy Graham's beaver dams, or of blowing up Billy for that matter. The linchpin of the agreement: Bucky would trap five live beavers and give them to Billy for the purpose of rebuilding the beaver dam, thus providing a haven for any more fingerling rainbow trout that Billy might want to nurture and cultivate.

Judge Patti's mouth fell open, but when she didn't detect a smile pasted across the face of either the parties or of me, she just shook her head, took the plea and entered the order. Within the next few of weeks, Bucky had managed to trap the elusive aqua-rodents. The critters were delivered by Bucky to Billy in a solemn ceremony one fine morning behind the courthouse in the parking lot, with a deputy, one well-scarred beaver hound of Bucky's, with Judge Patti witnessing the fruition of the great Beaver Restitution Order, a judicial command worthy of mention in the same breath as any solution ever achieved by Solomon.

The Court's Order approving this means of satisfying both Billy Graham's grievance with Bucky as well as the community's sense of justice was proposed by two willing parties, Bucky and Billy, recommended by a duly authorized member–to–be of the State Bar and executive branch (me), and set forth, accepted and approved by a democratically elected member of the judiciary – Judge Patti. Damn, isn't America a great country!

Hauling Ass in Shelby County

But there was one case that drew more media attention, some of it national, than any other with which I was personally involved during my entire tenure in the Shelby County District Attorney's Office. It was a misdemeanor cruelty to animals' case and it had the right blend of facts and characters to capture the imagination of the media and then the general public. Murder prosecutions, unless they are particularly heinous or otherwise notorious, are a dime a dozen and usually merit no more than about a paragraph's worth of printer's ink in the local rag. But kill, or be cruel to an animal, and the general populace, fed by the lurid details provided by the media, goes nuts. I give you Michael Vick as State's Exhibit One.

In this particular atrocity, a couple of half-drunk good ole boys had purchased a donkey and were proceeding back to the farm with it. Unfortunately for the donkey, and ultimately for the good ole boys, they simply put the poor creature on the bed of their pickup truck. They did secure the tailgate of the truck to prevent the poor relation to a fine horse from just walking out the rear of the truck. They made a much bigger mistake by tethering the animal with about twenty or thirty feet of rope which they attached to the donkey by a bit they had inserted into its mouth, with the other end of the rope secured in some fashion to the cab of the truck.

It was a disaster waiting to happen. And sure enough, as they were traveling about sixty mph down Highway 280, which connected Jefferson and Shelby counties, the donkey jumped over the side of the pick-up and the two good ole boys dragged it about one quarter mile on its side before they noticed that they were absent a passenger. Horrified onlookers driving by in their cars got the description of the truck, which they provided ASAP to the Sheriff's

Department. But one sharp-eyed pedestrian who just happened to be walking down the highway, probably trying to hitch a ride, managed to either memorize, or jot down, the tag number. Ultimately, the miscreants were arrested, the donkey was saved by a local veterinarian and the Shelby County Animal Shelter, and all that remained was to hang the good ole boys by the yardarm. That is to say, after they had received their "fair trial."

And so, all that remained was the hoorah preceding the trial, numerous media reports on the donkey and his progress in recovering from having the skin on one of his flanks essentially rubbed off by the asphalt of Highway 280, and of course, the trial and anticipated convictions. Ultimately the bad guys indeed were tried and convicted and were sent off to where bad guys are sent off, and all was well in Shelby County as well as Mudville, even though the Mighty Casey had struck out years before.

One funny remark which emerged from the proceedings was uttered by my good friend and beer drinking buddy, criminal defense attorney Mickey Johnson, who hailed from an unincorporated, and almost uninhabitable piece of real estate in the county known as "Fungo Holler." And don't ask me how it got its name. I saw Mickey at the courthouse several days after the trial, and his greeting to me was as follows: "Damn, Bob, if draggin' your ass in Shelby County is such a heinous crime, you and I are in big trouble." And that, among many other reasons is why I love Mickey Johnson to this day.

Oh, yes, the title to this book and how it became the title remains for me to explain.

A footnote to the sharp-eyed pedestrian who was the State's key witness at trial: His courtroom attire consisted of blue jeans and a T shirt which had printed across the front of it the title to the

Hank Williams Jr. song, "Whiskey Bent and Hell Bound." Within a month of giving his impassioned testimony, from which it was obvious he held people who are cruel to animals in the lowest possible regard, he was arrested for capital murder. He had run down an older man – several times – with his truck. I can't recall what the motive for this particular murder was, but I wouldn't be surprised if the old man held little or no abiding affection for donkeys. Feel free to draw whatever inferences you please from that turn of events. And so it went in Shelby County.

THE ANGEL OF DEATH, SHERIFF MORRIS AND JUDGE HUCKLEBERRY

THE UNFORGETTABLE CHARACTERS OF the Eighteenth Judicial Circuit (Shelby, Coosa and Clay Counties) were by no means limited to the litigants. One of the greatest – certainly one of the most memorable – was a District Court Judge from Coosa County, Robert Teel, Jr. Judge Teel, or the "Angel of Death" as he was affectionately known to us, was one of those individuals who was rather unprepossessing at first blush, particularly when he wasn't wearing his regal black finery, sitting on his judicial throne while surveying his kingdom. But slip that black dress on him and put him behind the bench, and he suddenly became a force with which to be reckoned.

The transformation of someone who looked more like an assistant clerk in the probate judge's office to a gavel wielding, ass-kicking, sho"nuff JUDGE, was a metamorphosis comparable to few other phenomena of nature. Perhaps the turning of a very plain caterpillar emerging from its cocoon into a beautiful butterfly is the closest that nature can come to replicating the change from Casper the Friendly Ghost to the Angel of Death. A better metaphor would be Lon Chaney, Jr. growing a little "hairy" at the sight of the next full moon.

His father, Robert Teel, Sr. was a practicing attorney in Rockford, county seat of Coosa, a former state legislator, and owner of anything worth owning in Coosa County – lock, stock and tomahawk. His brother, and his daddy's law partner, Frank Teel, was a patrician looking young Atticus Finch who had strikingly handsome features and enough Southern gentility to charm a bluebird from a dogwood tree. Together, he and his dad pretty much called the shots and made the big plays in the fourth quarter in Coosa County.

Bobby Teel had enough street smarts to know when (and how far) to depart from the black letter of the law and administer a modicum of "Teel's Law" when circumstances dictated its invocation. An occasional departure from the Code Of Alabama was easily understood and accepted by the local boys from the sawmill who got a little too drunk after work on occasion, and celebrated their good feelings by committing mutual ass whuppin' on each other. Bobby's law was much more effective than most of the drivel passed by the Montgomery Social Club, also known as the State Legislature. He had a sense of humor as dry as a double Martini during a vermouth drought at a James Bond film festival. And did I mention that he was also a bridge master? It was said that he could bid better than a bleached-blonde waitress at a yard sale, piecing together a bedroom suite for the family double wide.

Judge Teel traveled on a monthly basis from Rockford to Columbiana for the purpose of handling all of the child support cases. If you were not too far in arrears and appeared to be working earnestly to meet your legal obligations to provide monetary support for the next generation of litigants, ne'er-do-wells and defendants, Judge Teel was very fair and gave you every opportunity to meet your obligations. But if you lied to him, or if you'd taken the money that was supposed to pay for food and clothing for your offspring, the "Angel of Death" would come swooping down and inflict carnage of a sort not seen since Pickett's Charge at Gettysburg. It was ugly. It was horrifying. It was swift, and it was absolutely effective.

I once witnessed the good judge patiently listen to the sad tale of a deadbeat dad about not being able to find a job, not being able to make even a token payment for the support of his child, and how he would keep trying despite all of the obstacles that society had placed in his path to do right by his child. It truly was touching to listen to soft-spoken and avuncular Judge Teel tell the man that he understood the difficulties that good men sometimes just couldn't overcome. Bobby Teel urged this poor soul to just keep on keepin' on, and maybe he could come up with a bus token or two for his child by next month's docket.

I must confess that I momentarily lost faith in the Angel, and in his legendary ability to squeeze child support from the clenched fist and stiffening fingers of a dead man, even as the body was cold and Momma was squallin'. My brief lapse of unquestioning belief was answered by the Angel with a roar. The chosen sacrificial lamb of the month froze in his tracks and did his damndest to become invisible. But God's instrument was not to be denied; his voice shook the glass in the window panes and the fillings in my teeth. "DON'T TAKE ANOTHER STEP, YOU PREVARICATING TOAD!"

The anger and disgust virtually dripped from the Angel's lips. And the *Guess Jeans* label on the rear end of this moron's pants shone like a beacon across the sky on the night of a full moon. The poor, dumb slob who was the object of the AOD's (Angel, etc.) wrath had committed the mortal sin of wearing designer jeans to child support court, and then claiming that he couldn't make his payments because life hadn't been fair to him. Judge Teel then gave him just a small taste of how cruel life really *could* be, when one was stupid and/or arrogant enough to tug on Superman's cape, particularly when that cape was a black judicial robe worn by the AOD himself. Judge Teel ordered that the bailiff take the chiseler into custody and lock him up in our still fairly new jail until the man became current in his payments.

At the time, I wondered how he was to become current in his payments if he was sitting in jail with no visible means of supporting himself, not to mention his baby, but I was inexperienced and naïve, two failings with which the Death Angel was not afflicted. I didn't have long to wait for an answer to my unspoken question. That very day before the sun set on the cell of the scofflaw, his momma, his girl friend, and several other parties whose identities were otherwise unknown to the Sheriff, came straggling in with enough cash to buy freedom for the stupidity- stricken con man who wore designer jeans to Robert Teel's child support docket, as well as to take care of his child support arrearage.

Almost immediately after "Mr. Toad" was carted off by the Death Angel's bailiff, money from the other sad sacks on the docket poured in like justice rolling down like water. We collected more arrearage in child support payments that day than my younger son has excuses for why he can't finish his homework. I was just green enough to wonder whether Judge Bobby Teel was uncommonly lucky or exceedingly devious. Of course, as I eventually concluded, the entire performance had been orchestrated by the Angel of Death who knew that there was more than one way to skin a deadbeat dad for the good of the little chi'ren (pronounced cheer-en) and their frustrated mommas. Chalk one up for the benefits of deviousness in doing God's work.

Clay County was the third county in the Eighteenth Judicial Circuit and, in many ways, the most pleasant. Ashland, the county seat, was the hometown of a young Hugo Black, famed in later life for being a champion of the First Amendment as a United States Supreme Court Justice, and somewhat notorious for being a Ku Klux Klansman earlier in his career. Mr. Justice Black had practiced law in the courthouse, which was located in the town square, replete with benches where a few ageless men could always be found talking with each other while they whittled oak branches with their Barlow knives. The entire scene could have been lifted straight from the pages of To Kill a Mockingbird.

There was a young lawyer in Ashland, now a circuit judge recently defeated in a bid to become an Alabama Supreme Court Justice, who fashioned himself, if not as the reincarnation of Justice Black, at least as the guardian of Black's legacy, and as role model for his own judicial and historical destiny. Young John Rochester grew up among the lawyers, judges, clerks and court reporters who plied their trade at the courthouse, and, according to those who watched him develop during his days as a bootblack for the lawyers and judges, knew early on exactly what he wanted to be and how he was going to get there. God and the ghost of Hugo Black help anyone who posed a possible obstacle to his realizing his dream.

Johnny Rochester looked fourteen years old, an appearance that was highlighted by his shock of red hair that would put Bozo the Clown to shame, as well as by a minefield of freckles spattered from his brow to his chin. One could not help but think when first meeting him that Huckleberry Finn had been reincarnated in this friendly and enterprising young man. As a politician, he was one of the best campaigners I have ever seen work a room, or talk with a constituent one-on-one. He was as smooth as a flat river rock lifted from an ice cold brook in the Smokies and he never forgot a name. Looks, however, can deceive. When Johnny played politics, he played for keeps, and he had the memory of an elephant for any slight– real or perceived – to his person, or impediment to his political plans.

Years ago, a good friend of mine ran for circuit court judge in the Eighteenth Circuit, then consisting of Shelby, Coosa and Clay Counties. Since that time, then and now- Democratic Judge Rochester, upon observing the population boom in North Shelby County – which was about seventy-five per cent Republican – importuned a powerful state legislator to introduce a bill which would separate Shelby from the other two counties, thus creating a new circuit and removing the growing Republican block of voters from his electoral concerns. Of course the bill passed into law since Judge Johnny had for years courted certain legislators against the day when he needed a favor. No one ever accused Johnny Rochester of being short-sighted.

But, I stray from the point I was attempting to make. Both my friend and then-lawyer "Huckleberry" Rochester were seeking the same position. One of the important political meetings in that Circuit was the Shelby County Fraternal Order of Police's Meet the Candidates Night. My friend had to attend a fund raiser that night, one which had been scheduled weeks before the FOP had announced the date of their big political night. Since I was a member of the FOP, he asked me to stand in for him. Naturally, I assured him that I would.

However, when I arrived at the lodge that evening, I discovered that the rules of the event had been changed from years past. No stand-ins for the candidates would be allowed to speak. This meant that anything the speckle-faced young barrister said would be unrebutted. As I feared, the silver-tongued mouthpiece from Ashland was at his charming best. But, being no rookie at this time in my career, when I saw an opening, I took it.

Most of what Candidate Huckleberry said was uncontroversial and standard fare for a campaign speech. But then he made a crack about my friend's absence, and I just had to respond. During the period after each speech where the candidate fields questions, I stood and, instead of asking a question, very briefly explained to the crowd that my friend was attending a major fund-raising event that was scheduled long before the FOP's Meet the Candidates Night. And that was it.

From the stony silence which followed my announcement, you would have thought that I'd either relieved myself on Robert E. Lee's grave or farted while sitting in the front pew of the Resurrection Baptist Church. When all of the candidates had been introduced and gave their totally forgettable campaign spiels, I headed for the door that led to the parking lot. I glanced to my left and witnessed the next judge of the Eighteenth Judicial Circuit burning holes with his laser eyes right through me.

Mental Note to Myself: Don't ever again wave a red flag in front of a man running for judge, particularly one who has mapped out his career for the next thirty years. Perhaps fifteen years after that incident, another friend of mine told me that Judge Johnny still bites ten penny nails in half at the mere mention of my name. Oh well, perhaps he'll get over it before he becomes the next Hugo Black. If not, he'll just pay for a great deal of dental work, therapy and Prozac.

Since I have at least semi-retired, the chances of my running into Judge Huckleberry in his arena, that being a courtroom on the opposite side of the bench from me, are greatly diminished. And I'm certain that such an ardent admirer of Hugo Black – champion of free speech – would never allow his personal feelings about anyone simply exercising his First Amendment rights, to cloud his judgment in his capacity as a jurist. I also believe in blind trusts and the Easter Bunny.

Truth be told, Judge Rochester, despite taking himself and his position on the bench a little too seriously on occasion, has proved himself to be an astute jurist who likely would have been elected to the State Supreme Court had he only run as a Republican. Stay tuned to see whether Judge Huckleberry hops aboard that big gray elephant or continues to ride that Democratic donkey. If he aspires to any state-wide office, he'd better undergo a political metamorphosis or be content with retiring as a circuit court judge.

The High Sheriff of Clay County when I worked in that Circuit was Billy Morris. He was always pleasant to me, but I heard more than one person refer to him as "the meanest man alive". He was tall – at least 6' 2" – and weighed about 200 lbs. Word was that he had been an MP when he served in the Army, and had busted more than a few heads with his billy club, but only to effect a safe arrest when trouble reared its ugly head, which was more than once, according to my sources. One story which was told to me as being the unvarnished truth involved Sheriff Morris, and is too good not to be told, even if it is apocryphal. It seems that an arrest warrant was outstanding on a particular individual, whose name escapes me, but shall hereafter be known as Lee Roy. Lee Roy and his several brothers all lived with their Pa, and all had managed to cross swords with Sheriff Morris in the past.

The Sheriff's Posse, otherwise known as his Deputies, had been to Lee Roy's daddy's house on several occasions in vain attempts to effect Lee Roy's arrest. Ultimately, they returned to the Clay County Jail with a prisoner in tow. The prisoner, however, was not Lee Roy, but one of his brothers who we shall call Billy Bob. No, he hadn't done anything to merit an arrest, but he was the closest warm body to Lee Roy available to the Posse. Thus, a hostage was taken and this story has become legend.

After a period of a day or two, Lee Roy's father escorted Lee Roy to the lockup for the great prisoner exchange. Perhaps not as dramatic as the exchange in Berlin during the Cold War when the U.S. traded Soviet spymaster Rudolf Able for U2 pilot Francis Gary Powers, but the principle was the same. The deal was done, and none of the parties involved thought it unusual in any fashion. Remarkably, the entire transaction was viewed by Lee Roy, his father and Billy Bob, the brother who had spent some unearned time in the Clay County Cooler, as nothing more than the price of ignoring the law, as it was applied in Clay County, Alabama by Sheriff Morris and his minions. No doubt that the ACLU, had they been aware of this most serious violation of Billy Bob's rights, would have had a hissy fit. As would the FBI once their agents stopped laughing.

But, no harm, no foul. And life continued in Ashland, safe from the interference of "outside agitators," to resurrect an old phrase from a time, and in a place, where the Klan once rode high in the saddle. Sheriff Morris later was defeated in an election, but I doubt that his reign as High Sheriff was terminated by the voters for any reason remotely connected to the great hostage taking. He probably just didn't attend enough Bar-B-Qs or funerals prior to the election.

Chapter Two

MURDER: LIFE MAY BE CHEAP, BUT THE PRICE OF POKER RARELY IS!

WE DIDN'T TRY MANY cases in the Eighteenth Judicial Circuit for a variety of reasons, some good, others less so. But regardless of the reasons, the fact remained that normally, only very high profile cases were tried, and they were reserved for the District Attorney himself. Of course, one or more of the assistants sat "second chair" and usually examined a few witnesses and gave one of the two closing prosecution arguments. By October of 1983 when I left the jurisdiction to test the murky judicial waters of Mobile County, I had assisted in trying exactly two cases, which was about one third of all the cases tried in the three-county circuit during my tenure in that office. One of the two cases was an eminently forgettable BRCSP (Buying, Receiving and Concealing Stolen Property) case, but the other was a nice little murder case.

The summer after my second year in law school when I was working as an unpaid law clerk in the District Attorney's office, I had the opportunity to observe the trying of two other murder cases, one of them capital, which could not be described as anything other than mean and evil. Both of those cases were tried in the summer of 1980, one in Shelby County, the second in Coosa County. Each resulted in a conviction, one defendant receiving a life sentence, the second the death penalty.

In the Shelby case, Bobby Joe Hope, together with his brother Phillip, had drowned their cousin, Louie Earl Jones, reportedly because he stole Bobby Joe's tool box and the tools inside the box. That seemed to Bobby Joe and his brother Phillip sufficient reason to impose the death penalty. And Louie Earl didn't have to sit on death row for twenty years awaiting imposition of sentence. As far as the Shelby County Supreme Court of the Hope brothers was concerned, it was *cert* denied, and the deed was done. And the brothers themselves could be, and subsequently were paroled, to the best of my memory. But before I proceed with the details of that trial, allow me to give you a preview of coming attractions.

In July of 1979 in Coosa County, just outside of Rockford, the county seat, Timothy Charles Davis brutally robbed, sexually assaulted and then murdered Avis Alford, a grandmotherly lady, known and respected throughout the community. He stabbed her in the back numerous times while she lay naked on the floor, totally humiliated, scared beyond belief and no doubt writhing in agony until death mercifully took her. Davis was tried and convicted a year after the murder and sentenced to die in the electric chair. And, but for the intervention of the United States Supreme Court, he would still likely be waiting for execution more than a quarter century after his heinous crime. Before I shock you with more details of Davis's crime and his subsequent conviction, I'll tell you a bit about the other two murder cases that I observed or helped to try during my tenure in Columbiana.

Shotgun Shootin' in a Double-Wide and Shot Glasses on a Verdict Watch

THE ONE THAT I helped my boss and one of the other ADAs to try was the less than memorable case of the <u>State of Alabama</u> v. <u>Hulon Wilson. Hulon was</u> a poor wretch who finally got fed up with his trailer mate's bullying and probably very aggressive homosexual ways. He sought permanent injunctive relief from whatever indignities and buggery that Jim Davis visited on him. The injunction was granted by Wilson himself, and was permanent in that it relieved Mr. Davis of the trouble of living. The injunction was derived from some ancient extrapolation of the English Common Law and "No Law West of the Pecos" known as "shotgun relief." This remedy was similar to the common form of the dissolution of a marriage in Texas, the ever popular "Smith and Wesson" divorce. What Hulon Wilson did was to deliver a load of buckshot at point blank range into Jim Davis.

The authorities, responding to Wilson's timely notification of the elimination of his tormentor, found Davis in the narrow hallway of the double wide. His body was on its knees, forehead touching the floor, and there was still a half-smoked cigarette smoldering between the fingers of his right hand. The blood spatters on the walls of the trailer were measured at no higher than about thirty-eight to forty inches above the floor. Neither Sherlock Holmes nor Dr. Henry Lee had to be called in to interpret the physical evidence in this killin'. The plain view of the crime scene itself pretty much spelled out what had happened.

It was obviously an execution, and I surmised that Hulon was tired of being Jim Davis's bitch. But Wilson and his attorneys decided to take their chances by drawing to an inside straight, rarely a good move to make either in poker or in a murder trial. Male pride being what it is, however, Hulon never would admit to anything, other than to offer the rather lame explanation that Davis somehow attacked him, and Hulon just happened to have his shotgun loaded and at the ready. In order to explain the angle of entry of the buckshot, which was absolutely consistent with Davis being on his knees and the shooter being no more than about three feet away, standing over Davis with the shotgun pointed at his chest, his lawyers took the only tack available to them; they tried to make chicken salad out of chicken droppings. And they did a damned good job of taking that sow's ear and nearly making a silk purse of it.

They got the pathologist to admit that the angle of entry of the buckshot depended on the relative positions of the two bodies. Then they suggested that Davis made a run at Wilson, diving at him when Hulon defended himself by firing the shotgun, and that that scenario possibly could explain the angle of entry of the buckshot. This explanation, aside from barely passing the laugh test, also conveniently omitted any reference to the smoldering cigarette being clasped between Davis's fingers as his body lay slumped over in the tripod position – head and both knees flat on the floor.

But Hulon Wilson, if nothing else, was a pathetic and pitiful excuse for a human being. He was an underweight, malnourished, shriveled up and tubercular looking throw-away chap, who would not be mourned or missed by society. By contrast, at least to a certain extent, the very late Jim Davis was younger looking, better nourished and somewhat fit – at least before Hulon Wilson ruined his day, not to mention his entire mid-section. There was no question but that the jury would feel sorry for the defendant and not sympathetic in the slightest toward the so-called victim. And it's in just such cases that a jury needs no more than the frailest of pegs to find reasonable doubt and return a verdict of "Not Guilty". But sometimes, the physical evidence is just a little too strong for even a sympathetic jury to ignore. This hummer turned out to be one of those cases.

After the judge charged the jury as to the law, all of the lawyers – defense included – repaired to the D.A.'s office to await the verdict. Normally, a judge will adjourn court and dismiss a jury from their deliberations at a time certain – 5:00 P.M. was the normal time to quit for the evening in Shelby County. For whatever reason, the judge in this trial wanted a verdict before the next day, if at all possible. And so, all of us presumed that there would be a verdict within an hour or two. Boy, were we ever wrong!

To pass the time while waiting for a verdict, the Chief Deputy suggested that each of us, defense attorneys included, might want to have a libation or two in order to preserve the air of civility that we enjoyed, notwithstanding our respective roles as advocates in opposition to each other. I made a quick trip to the local liquor store and purchased some fine, aged Jack Daniels. Of course, no one wanted to go out to eat – nothing was open in Columbiana at that hour anyway, so we shared some stale Ritz crackers, and chased the crackers with that smooth, brown liquid from Lynchburg, Tennessee.

Time passed, my adrenaline was in overdrive, and the Jack Daniels seemed to have a calming effect on me. In another setting, I would likely refer to that calming effect as being drunk as an Irishman in Boston on St. Patty's Day. But, after about seven hours of passing the time being civilized, if not entirely civil or sober, we got the call from the bailiff that the verdict knock on the jury room door finally had echoed through the nearly empty courtroom. I weaved and wobbled my way into the courtroom along with the other advocates for justice who, having been there before – taken a verdict, that is – had been somewhat more circumspect than I in their consumption of the nectar of the gods.

Our office investigator, Bob O'Connor, about whom more will be said later, saw the potential for trouble in my state of greatly reduced sobriety, and made certain that he sat directly behind me in the courtroom. His prescience possibly saved me from a night in my own cell, courtesy of the court. I had a foreboding that the jury felt sympathetic enough toward Hulon to cut him loose, and thus was more than slightly and pleasantly surprised when I heard the foreman pronounce that magical word "Guilty" when he read the verdict form.

And it was only because Robby O' was attuned enough to the state of my fading and fuzzy mind that he headed me off at the pass. Because as soon as that last syllable left the foreman's lips, I was restrained from jumping straight out of my chair only by the strong hands of Mr. O' Connor set firmly on each of my shoulders. Unfortunately, he lacked a third hand to place over my mouth. Saying "No shit," at counsel table, even in a stage whisper as I did, is not usually smiled at by even the most benevolent of judges. Telfair Mashburn, a visiting judge from Mobile, and in whose courtroom I would later try cases when I made the move to the Port City, had a habit of occasionally turning off his hearing aid. Apparently, he had chosen just that minute to turn it off, because he never even blinked at my grievous breach of decorum.

In life, as in poker, timing is everything. And poor Hulon turned out to have fortune smile upon him within the next year. After Judge Mashburn sentenced him to a life term in the big house, the Court of Criminal Appeals reversed the conviction on a totally bogus interpretation of Alabama case law. On remand for a new trial, Hulon pled guilty to an offer of manslaughter with a sentence of far less than life. Apparently the good judges felt more empathy for the plight of Hulon Wilson than did the jury. At least they didn't apologize to him and order that his shotgun be returned to him after he had been "rehabilitated" at Draper Prison.

The Hulon Wilson case was the first murder trial that I actually helped to prosecute. But as I mentioned earlier in my mental meanderings, there were two murder cases that I observed being tried during the summer of 1980 when I was an unpaid clerk and about to begin my third and final year of law school. Both of these cases were of a sort that gave murder a bad name. That statement may upset some people who are of a mind that all murders are equally bad, morally indefensible and/or likely to result in the murderer condemning himself for all eternity to the fiery nether regions after standing before that final court of appeals presided over by the Deity Himself. Working in law enforcement for any appreciable length of time will cure any innocent soul of that misguided notion forever.

Except for the belief, which I happen both to endorse and subscribe, that every person has an immortal soul and the same intrinsic worth as any other human being, the fact remains that some people simply are worth more than others. The death of one might be a tragedy while the death of the other could evoke no more feeling than that produced when stepping on a cockroach. You're shocked? Appalled? Thanking God that you could never become as jaded and lacking in basic morals as a retired prosecutor who obviously never should be trusted in civilized society? Well, murder may always be morally wrong, but you can't really equate the winner in a barroom knife fight with the evil of oh, let's say, Adolph Hitler. Of course that's an extreme example. But there are literally uncountable numbers of similar contrasts between people you have never met, and those whose names you have never heard uttered.

As a prosecutor, I have taken an oath to protect the innocent and to ferret out the guilty, and I don't give oaths lightly. But I never took an oath that I would be equally sympathetic to all victims of crimes. Sometimes, the only difference between a victim and a defendant is who could shoot better or faster. The examples of Hulon Wilson and Jim Davis come to mind rather quickly. Davis didn't deserve his fate, and Wilson certainly wasn't justified in his role of self-appointed judge, jury and executioner. But, as murders go, neither man evoked much sympathy from the community.

No Hope for the Hopes

TIMOTHY CHARLES DAVIS AND Bobby Lee Hope were another breed of cat, however. Hope was cold and mean; Davis was just one evil son-of-a-bitch who should have been drowned at birth. I know that I personally would have taken my turn at the water bucket without flinching. Hope and his brother Phillip were charged with murder for drowning their cousin, Louie Earl Jones in a local creek. Louie Earl had stolen Bobby Joe's tool box, which contained well over $100 worth of new tools. At least Bobby Joe believed that Louie Earl was the thief. After Bobby Joe and Phillip had finished holding their cousin's head under water, Louie Earl's lungs would be so filled with the muddy brown liquid meandering slowly down that little tributary of the Cahaba River that the only tool of any use to him would be a good pump.

I can't remember precisely when Louie Earl Jones met his maker, but I'm relatively certain that it also was that summer of 1978. I do know, however, that both Hope and Davis were tried in the summer of 1980, Hope in June and Davis in July. Bobby Joe's brother, Phillip, had been tried and convicted before Bobby Joe, but my best recollection is that his conviction was reversed on appeal, and that either he was convicted again or pled guilty his second time at bat. Bobby Joe, however, said "prove it" and insisted on his constitutional right to be tried by a jury of his peers.

There were a couple of things that stood out at trial, even more so than the testimony which was chilling enough. The first was the appearance of Bobby Joe himself. He was strikingly handsome, and had a body that appeared chiseled from granite. But he was so cold that the room temperature seemed to drop ten degrees whenever the deputies brought him in from his cell. "Bad to the bone" is what comes to mind when picturing Bobby Joe Hope in my rogues' gallery of mean dudes.

But even Bobby Joe wasn't as bad as at least one other fellow from the south end of Shelby County. And that would be Mr. J.W. Carden. J.W. must have been the model for Jimmy Dean's hit record, "Big John". That memorable tune celebrated a mythical coal miner who, after a cave-in one morning at the mine, supported a broken beam with his back, allowing his buddies to escape with their lives. "Big John stood 6'6" and weighed 245," went the lyrics to the hit tune of 1961. J.W. wasn't quite six and a half feet tall, but he sure looked it, and he carried at least 245 lb. of raw-boned, country strong muscle. Bobby Joe may have resembled a panther with his sinewy muscles appearing as if they had been painted over his taut skin, but J.W. was a full grown grizzly bear with the disposition of one who's been wounded and is dead set on inflicting a little pain himself.

Aside from the fact that J.W. Carden was a man's man and a thoroughly impressive and intimidating presence, there is another reason that I tell you about him. And that reason is that his history with Hope made it worth the price of admission to attend Bobby Joe's murder trial that summer of 1980. It seems that sometime in the not too distant past, before Bobby Joe and Phillip Hope baptized their cousin Louie Earl Jones to the extent that he never recovered from ingesting so much water in his lungs, Bobby Joe and J.W. "got into it" as they say, at Lib's, a juke joint on the river. Lib's was one of those places where you didn't go unless you either were lookin' to kick some ass or to get yours kicked.

As I understand it, on this particular occasion, J.W. stomped on old Bobby Joe like nobody ever had before that occasion. Anybody but Bobby Joe Hope would have been discouraged from escalating the war. But Bobby Joe didn't take too kindly to having his ass so thoroughly kicked. Rather than exercise the better part of valor, he chose instead to finish both it and J.W. by fetching his "Roscoe" and emptying it into the big man. Anybody but J.W. Carden would have taken up a temporary residence on a slab in the coroner's office in Birmingham before being planted "'neath the green, green grass of home." But J.W. was no ordinary man, and it would take more than six shells from a .38 Special to finish him off.

When Hope came to trial for this particular transgression – attempted murder and assault first degree, I believe, J.W. refused to identify Hope, or simply said that Hope didn't do it, leaving the State with no choice but to dismiss the case. For all who were present in court that day, there wasn't much doubt as to what J.W. had planned for Bobby Joe Hope. But then an intervening factor changed the likely course of events. Louie Earl Jones went and got himself drowned by the Hope brothers, and they both were arrested shortly thereafter. Thus, J.W. Carden had to put aside his apparent plan to exact his own brand of personal justice on Bobby Joe Hope.

But he just couldn't keep himself from attending Hope's murder trial, and every day of the trial, before proceedings began, J.W. would report dutifully to the District Attorney's office and hand over his "piece" to our office investigator. Bob O'Connor would maintain possession of it until after the close of testimony each day until Bob-by Joe had been returned to his cell by the deputies. Mr. Carden sat in the front pew in the courtroom every day of the trial. When the foreman of the jury read the guilty verdict, two almost indiscernible things happened: Bobby Joe's face flushed ever so slightly, the only emotion he displayed during the entire trial, and just a suggestion of a smile appeared on the face of J.W. Carden. After retrieving his gun from our investigator, he left the courthouse and never looked back.

An interesting aside to the saga of the Hope brothers is their father, Hubert, and what he attempted to do to avenge his boys. Hubert Hope was a former Shelby County Deputy Sheriff, but he didn't let the weight of the badge that he'd worn for a number of years get in the way of his own personal morality and set of laws. Chief among his prohibitions was allowing *anyone* to mess with his family. Right, wrong or confused, you did *not want* to face Hubert if you had wronged a member of his family. And whether that family member was in the right or otherwise, wasn't really relevant as to how Hubert viewed his duty to teach you a lesson.

And Old Hubert took those lessons very seriously, as serious as a heart attack or a double Jack Daniels on an empty stomach. Thus it was in the summer of 1981, about a year after the trial, that I picked up the newspaper one morning after two or three cups of coffee before starting to study for the bar exam. The glaring headlines on the front page just about jumped up and bit me. Hubert Hope had been arrested for soliciting a state prisoner to murder Billy Hill, the District Attorney. Hill had been the chief prosecutor of Bobby Joe the summer before Hubert went looking for payback.

Hubert, however, made the classic mistake of the amateurs who seek to have a spouse, business partner or someone who has crossed them, "sleep with the fishes" as they say in *La Cosa Nostra*. He contacted a stranger and offered him money to do, or to arrange, the "hit". The person that he contacted was a state prisoner named Jesse Jett, who apparently had a reputation within the "system" of being someone who could "make things happen."

Of course, what Jesse Jett actually did to stay comfortable behind the prison walls was to be a con man and an excellent snitch for "the man" And thus, he reported faithfully to his masters at the prison about Hope's approach to him, etc. And they took it from there. That summer of 1981 my sole goal in life was to study sufficiently for the bar exam, in order that I pass it the first time around the block. Thus, I was not working as a clerk that summer, and didn't learn of the plot to assassinate my boss until after the trap had been sprung and the news hit the papers.

And Hope's lust for revenge ran so hot and so fast that he didn't limit himself to knocking off just Billy Hill. His ambitions drove him to come up with a list of all those who had crossed him. That is to say, all those who did their duty by prosecuting his sons were members of this elite club. That list included former Deputy District Attorney Patti Smith who by this time was a district court judge, as well as former District Attorney, and now Circuit Court Judge Harold Walden for prosecuting Phillip Hope for his role in the murder of Louie Earl Jones. And lest I forget, the list also included Alabama Attorney General Charles Graddick for providing an experienced murder prosecutor to assist Billy Hill during Bobby Joe's trial. I extend my apologies to anyone who made the cut for the final roster on the "hit" parade, but whom I have neglected to mention. My memory isn't quite what it used to be.

Fortunately, Hubert Hope was arrested before he could execute his plan to execute those on the list. But not before most of them had a few anxious days wondering whether all of the protection provided to them was sufficient. It was. And Hubert Hope ended up pleading guilty to Solicitation to Commit Murder and spent several years behind bars until the State Board of Pardons and Paroles made a determination that the old reprobate no longer posed a threat to anyone. Nobody has made an attempt to murder any of the people on the list as far as I know. I'm just proud to be here and not on any list of Hubert Hope. I did make it on another list after I became a fed, but Marvin Holley is now doing life without parole in the federal joint for murdering a witness in a drug trial. Marvin is very determined, but fortunately, also very stupid. You will learn much more about him when I write a second book about my years as a "Fed."

Young Manson

Timothy Charles Davis didn't restrict his murdering ways to relatives, or to men for that matter. His victim was Avis Alford, a very nice lady by all accounts, who ran a mom and pop grocery store and filling station just off a county road in Coosa County. Young Tim, then seventeen years old in the summer of 1978, but married and working full time, had to make a payment on his motorcycle which was due the day after he robbed Ms. Alford of her money, her dignity and her life. His solution for raising quick money was to wield his knife as his chosen instrument of death, and to take the money from the cash register at the mom and pop.

And, yes, to rape and kill Ms Alford at her grocery store. And since no one else happened to be in the store that particular afternoon, at that particular time, why not just anally sodomize her and then stab her seventeen times in the back while still crouching over her? Mr. Davis apparently didn't have any further murderous activities planned for that afternoon, and so he just took his time robbing, degrading and killing Ms. Alford.

The robbery, sexual assault and murder occurred in the late afternoon. Davis's sexual assault of Mrs. Alford took place on the customer side of the counter. Her naked, lifeless body was discovered no more than half an hour after Davis had finished his handiwork. By working backwards from the time of the discovery of Mrs. Alford's body to the time she was last seen or heard from, investigators were able to fashion in short order a roughly accurate time line, vital in establishing an accurate time of death, and later, in checking alibis of possible suspects, scrutinizing who had the opportunity to do the crime.

I must say that the work of some Coosa County Deputies, together with several investigators from the Alabama Bureau of Investigation (ABI), was some of the best investigative work that I had heard of or seen during my twenty plus years as a prosecutor. Hell, if these boys had been with the L.A.P.D. in 1994, O.J. would never have beaten the rap. They first determined that the killer was left handed, based on the fact that all seventeen stab wounds were on the upper left quadrant of Mrs. Alford's back, and entered at an angle that made it virtually impossible that a person holding the knife in his right hand could inflict those wounds at such an angle. They then conducted a very careful search of the entire premises, inside and out, and did not recover a knife. By this time, a man who had been riding by the store at about the time of the murder, heard on the radio about the crime, turned his car around and drove to the little store.

When he arrived at the store, he reported to the Deputies and Investigators that while approaching the store at about the time of the murder, he saw a young man wearing a yellow plastic helmet riding toward him on a motorcycle, apparently having just left the parking area of the store. He reported to the investigators as to what he had seen, and they questioned him extensively as to whether he had seen anything in the man's hands. After they were satisfied that the motorcycle rider hand nothing in either hand, one of the investigators, Ronny Cribbs of the Alabama Bureau of Investigation, I believe, performed a bit of investigative legerdemain which would have done Sherlock Holmes proud.

Ronnie reasoned that because Mrs. Alford had been stabbed in the left-hand side of her back, and because of the angle of entry of the stab wounds, the killer must have been left handed. After questioning closely the man in the car who had driven by the store shortly after the murder, and after conducting a thorough search of the premises which turned up nothing of evidentiary value, Cribbs became convinced that the presumed killer was the young man riding the motorcycle. Based on the direction he was heading down the county road, as well as the fact that the driver of the car saw nothing in either hand of the motorcycle rider, Cribbs concluded that the biker / presumed killer had the knife in his left hand when he took off on his motorcycle, and then threw the knife into the field on his left just before the man in the car passed him going in the opposite direction. Sure enough, a search of the field with the aid of a metal detector yielded the murder weapon the next morning.

But by the time that investigators found the murder weapon the morning after Davis performed his handiwork on Mrs. Alford, he already was the main suspect. People not in law enforcement, particularly those who like to be thought of as a bit more intellectually sophisticated than your average bear, tend to pooh-pooh certain truisms of those in the business that chase bad guys. One of those truisms is that the criminal always returns to the scene of the crime.

A professional burglar or con man might be the exceptions to this maxim, but it never ceases to amaze cops and prosecutors how often amateur crooks – and they are the most dangerous to human life – follow that course of conduct, which often leads to their arrest and conviction.

Thank the Lord that T.C. Davis was just an amateur at his murderous trade. He showed up at the scene as police and spectators gathered, and he still had his yellow motorcycle helmet with him. And the helmet still had Mrs. Alford's spattered blood on it. What a genius! Then again, as many a prosecutor has told many a jury in rebuttal argument: "Folks, I don't want to disillusion any of you about the excellent police work that we had in this case, but the fact of the matter is that most of the crooks that we catch and later convict, aren't real candidates to receive academic honors upon graduating from Thug University."

An aging hobo (or "homeless person" for you of the school of political correctness) became the "real" killer according to the defense, when he was located. He had observed young Manson washing the blood from his hands in a nearby river tributary. That particular red herring never even got off the ground, much less take flight, at the trial. Whatever the defense was selling the jury wasn't buying. Davis was taken into custody on the day of the murder. Unbelievably, he was released following a hearing of some sort, perhaps an arraignment, or initial appearance. That hearing was conducted the day following his arrest, I believe. He quickly absconded to Georgia where he was apprehended after the judicial foul up was corrected.

The reference to "young Manson", however, fit T.C. Davis much better than the glove fit O.J. He had shoulder-length hair and wild, penetrating eyes resulting in an uncanny resemblance to Manson. At trial, even though he was cleaned up, wearing a coat and tie and sporting a fashionable cut of his previously stringy locks, his eyes and the way that he glided around the courtroom like a shark circling its prey, was not lost on the all female jury.

Davis was so enamored with his own celebrity that he insisted upon representing himself, albeit as co-counsel to a pair of seasoned criminal defense attorneys. He often would rise from the counsel table and move to the rear of the jury box, so as to better stare holes through a witness. The women in the jury box visibly cringed and shrank from his presence every time that he occupied that space. Needless to say, the prosecution never objected to his movements.

Numerous other items of evidence were recovered and introduced at trial that linked Davis to the worst murder in Coosa County history. Blood spatter testimony outlined in remarkable fashion TCD's method of murder and sodomy. An admission to a fellow juvenile inmate in the Georgia facility which was holding Davis didn't help Davis's cause when his cell buddy testified against him at trial.

Another piece of evidence, while not absolutely necessary, proved to be some of the icing on the cake given to the jury. Jimmy Abbot, the ABI investigator in charge of the case, made certain that he observed Davis taking notes during jury selection. Thus, he was able to testify that Davis, indeed, was left handed. As I said, a nice touch that served to tie up any loose ends.

One item of absolutely damning evidentiary value was a tape recorded statement that Davis had made to a counselor at the juvenile facility in Georgia. In that taped statement, Davis admitted what he had done to Ms. Alford, but the statement was ruled to be inadmissible because the counselor had not advised Davis of his right to remain silent. However, because the statement was made without coercion or duress being applied to Davis, the tape would be admissible if Davis were to testify and deny that he committed his terrible deeds. The tape could be used to rebut his lies. Thus, Davis did not have the opportunity to tell his lies to the jury.

The tape did, however, play an interesting role as a catalyst for probing Davis's warped psyche. The District Attorney, Billy Hill, decided to provide Mr. Davis with a final opportunity to plead guilty and receive a recommended sentence of life without parole. In order to accomplish that end, Davis's brother, a police officer from Columbus, Georgia had to be convinced of his brother's guilt. He refused to believe that his younger brother was capable of committing such a heinous act – until he heard the tape which was played for him in a private setting while the jury was at lunch, and before Judge Kenneth Ingram had instructed them as to the law. The brother broke down crying and then did his best, together with Davis's wife and also his mother, to persuade the murdering little coward to plead guilty and take the offer of life without possibility of parole.

I was able to observe the mini-drama which was played out in a witness room that conveniently had a glass square set in the wooden door, through which I was able to see it all and to hear most of it. I heard Davis say that he could not admit to what he had done because it would disgrace the family. His brother responded that he had already disgraced the family, but that he could still save his life. I remember watching Davis hyperventilate and then experience a severe nosebleed – presumably because his blood pressure had to be sky high by that time. Predictably, he turned down the offer and shortly thereafter was convicted of capital murder.

The all female jury returned a guilty verdict in less than forty-five minutes. Under Alabama law at that time, the jury was not told that the judge could sentence the defendant to life without parole. Thus, the jury was faced with the belief that a guilty verdict meant that the defendant would automatically receive the death penalty. This jury, despite some tears from several of its members, did not shirk its duty. At a later date, Judge Ingram sentenced Timothy Charles Davis to die in the electric chair. After the jury was dismissed by Judge Ingram, Billy Hill played for them the tape of Davis's confession. Any lingering doubts that they had done the right thing were erased by the playing of the tape.

TC Davis was a mere child of seventeen, married and working a full-time job when he committed his "youthful indiscretion." But, more than twenty years after his conviction, the United States Supreme Court in a five to four decision in another case decided that a person had to be at least eighteen years of age at the time of the capital offense in order to be subjected to the death penalty. Davis had not attained the magical age of eighteen when he did his evil deed that summer of 1979. And, of course, being a few months shy of his eighteenth birthday, he lacked the necessary judgment and maturity, as well as not having a sufficiently developed moral compass to be subjected to the death penalty, the imposition of which would make our more civilized allies in Europe like and appreciate us even less than they now do.

All of these considerations were now the *sine qua non* of his being able to fully understand the gravity of robbing an elderly lady at knife point, anally sodomizing her and then stabbing her in the back with the knife seventeen times until she bled to death. The majority of Supreme Court Justices found, in effect, that "evolving standards" of what a sovereign country might impose by way of punishment meant that no one who was less than eighteen years of age when he committed an act of savagery so brutal that it merited the ultimate penalty could now be subjected to that penalty because … well, because. To allow such a barbaric practice to continue would mean that people abroad might not like us. And once that floodgate was opened, our ambassadors might be stricken from the "A" list of foreign dignitaries on the diplomatic cocktail circuit. And what a tragedy that would be!

Almost twenty-five years after his conviction, Davis, (along with everyone else on death rows across the country who was less than eighteen at the time of their crimes), was given a reprieve by five weak – kneed weenies on the United States Supreme Court. Oh! In other words, the five members of the Court who joined in that decision decided that a seventeen-year-old lacked the basic judgment and conscience of the average mentally impaired ten-year-old. And executing such a person would simply be mean and vindictive. (The words are mine, not those of the Supremes.) The wheels of justice often grind so slowly as to be all but frozen in time. And sometimes, those wheels just come off the wagon. Thus, Timothy Charles Davis will merely spend the rest of his sorry life in an Alabama prison.

Funny, I've read the Constitution from Preamble through the Twenty-Seventh Amendment, and *apparently* I've missed that part which gives a myriad of powers to the judiciary that I previously thought were the purview of the Congress or of the states themselves. How wrong could I be? I guess this "revoltin' development" means a return to remedial reading for me. Either that or some heretofore unknown clause in the Constitution makes the Supreme Court the supreme ruler of the great unwashed masses. (Of which I am proudly one.) I can now only hope that Timothy Charles Davis lives a very long and totally miserable existence in his cage at whatever state prison in which he is designated to live out his days.

A footnote to this morality play is that the lying little bastard continues to maintain his innocence and apparently has convinced enough tools who choose to live in a different dimension of their own reality sufficient to inspire them to write poetry about Davis's "innocence" as well as to maintain their own distorted and false account of the evidence. Just Google "Timothy Charles Davis, capital murder," if you wish to see the unmitigated gall of these useful idiots, and why their scribblings simply undermine their opposition to the death penalty.

Most prosecutors would much prefer to see a person admit his wrongdoing and beg forgiveness than to actually be executed, however richly he might deserve the ultimate penalty.

And so it goes.

Chapter Three

The Heart of Darkness

By the summer of 1983, I had come to the realization that, if I wanted to be the biggest and meanest trial dog on the porch, I would have to move to a bigger porch with meaner dogs, just waiting for the next piece of live meat to maim and devour. After I'd pulled up stakes and left the tranquil hills and valleys of the Eighteenth Judicial Circuit, I made the big move to the Mobile County District Attorney's Office, the sole county in the Thirteenth Judicial Circuit.

And when I had moved to that bigger porch, I learned quickly that some of those defense attorneys were absolute pit bulls. I would come to experience their bites first hand. I soon learned how to inflict a few maulings of my own just in order to survive. Two of my friends, as well as being law school classmates of mine and Deputy District Attorneys in Mobile, had to crack the door enough for me to get an interview. That discussion with Joe Thetford and Bill Steele occurred in August. By late October I was trying cases in Mobile Circuit Court. Molly, my wife, put up with a weekend marriage until January when she gave up an excellent job in Shelby County, and secured a lesser paying one in Mobile. What a good woman will do for her man still astounds me.

Prior to my exodus to L.A. (Lower Alabama), I did some checking with our District Attorney's Investigator. He was a good Orangeman from Northern Ireland – at least his forbears were from Ulster – by way of Mobile - with the fine Irish name of Robert O'Connor, and about whom you have read earlier in this chapter. This was the same Robby O' who had saved me from myself when the verdict in the Hulon Wilson murder trial was read aloud. He may have been an infidel to my Church's way of thinking. But, by this time in my spiritual journey, my belief system ran more to the theology of George Carlin than it did to that of Thomas Aquinas. And Robby O's heart was in the right place.

His lovely wife Judy was a real iron magnolia from Selma, Alabama. She was a total sweetheart as well as being a lady with whom you wouldn't want to trifle. Judy was the chief probation officer in Shelby County and a crack pistol shot with better aim than just about any other law enforcement officer in the county. She was more than a match for the rascally Robby'O.

After Robby O' filled me in on where the skeletons were buried in the Port City – and I'm not just writing metaphorically – I wasn't at all certain that Mobile was the city in which I wanted to live and ply my trade. Besides being a garden spot for azaleas and magnolias, it proved to be a cornucopia of crime, as well as the front line for ambitious prosecutors. He also gave me an illustration of the difference between "old wealth" and "new wealth," stressing to me that Mobile was a city of "old wealth." "Robert", he said, "the difference between the two is that new wealth allows you to buy a loaf of bread. Old wealth enables you to hire a servant who will go into town to buy you a loaf of bread whenever you want one." Within a few short weeks of my having pulled stakes in Shelby County and pitched my tent in the Port City, I witnessed first hand exactly what O'Connor had told me.

I started to get an inkling of what I might be in for on my initial drive to Mobile. There is an exit from I-10 about forty miles from the city which leads to Gulf Shores, the "Redneck Riviera" of the Gulf Coast. Accurately named, although not too imaginatively, it is the Gulf State Parkway, and there is a filling station there that is visible from the interstate. I stopped there to gas up and recycle some coffee.

During a conversation with the manager, he asked me why I was headed to Mobile. When I told him that I hoped to be hired to work in the DA's Office as a prosecutor, he arched his brows a bit and wanted to know whether I was going down for anything related to the arrest of a major figure in law enforcement in neighboring Baldwin County for his role in a substantial marijuana deal a year or two prior to my trip south. When I assured him that I wasn't, he visibly relaxed.

Not that his relationship with the crooked lawman had anything to do with his changed and re-changed demeanor. He told me that he merely knew the man, and was certainly surprised that he would be involved in anything illegal. It's been said that I was born at night on the back of a turnip truck. That assertion might be true about the turnip truck, but it wasn't last night. I could only wonder what delights awaited me in the Port City when I was actually on the job. I was soon to find out.

My memory is somewhat hazy regarding that first visit to Mobile, the purpose of which was to be interviewed by Chris Galanos, the District Attorney, for the job as a Deputy District Attorney. However, I do recall that the interview occurred early in September, the week after Galanos was stopped for driving under the influence of prescription diet pills. That may sound pretty goofy – and it was – but it just marked the beginning of a very goofy time, even for Mobile. I'll get into all of that later. For now, I'll merely say that the one question that stands out in my mind about the interview was Galanos looking me in the eyes and asking me: "You know you might be climbing on board a sinking ship if I hire you, don't you?" I looked back at him and assured him that not only was I an excellent swimmer, but also a certified water safety instructor, a skill that might come in handy for the office if it was taking on water as fast as I had heard. He laughed, and I got the job.

Prior to my making the move several weeks later, I considered that, by reputation and generally held belief, Mobile simply was a city of the Old South, and couldn't have been the little Chicago that O'Conner had described to me. I was wrong; it was worse. The entire Gulf Coast from Galveston to Pensacola was simultaneously quiet and sleepy on the one hand, and absolutely wild, wooly and wicked on the other.

The term *Banana Republic* best describes the Mobile of 1983 when I moved there that fall. Not that it wasn't a pleasant place in which to live; merely politically primitive and socially ante-bellum. Business, politics, religion and society blended in such a fashion that any one couldn't be separated from the others. Nor could the law and ordinary rules of civil business proceedings adhered to in other, more developed cities on the urban evolutionary scale, be considered SOP in the Port City. Outsiders – that is residents abiding there for fewer than three generations – were tolerated but never embraced by "Old Mobile," or those who fell within the almost hallowed category of "fine old Mobile family." (FOMF)

Certain aspects of life in Mobile seem more than a tad incongruous when its facade is first examined. It is generally thought to be one of the few remaining strongholds of Old South gentility, manners and charm, much like Savannah, Georgia and Charleston,

South Carolina. I suppose a pretty good case could be made supporting that image, but I'd bet dollars to dollops of Cajun cookin' that I could make a stronger case that Mobile is also just a smaller version of New Orleans – a rollicking and rough seaport on the Gulf Coast filled with corruption, vice, violence and its own set of rules and customs for handling the flowers and weeds that grow from the rich soil of its two faces, the Chamber of Commerce image on one side of the coin, as well as the sleazy and seedy life which is merely the other side of the same coin.

After wilting on the vine for two years in the wilds of Shelby, Coosa and Clay Counties, I was just about desperate to head to more fertile ground for my development as the State's reincarnation of Clarence Darrow. This reincarnation, however, would wear the white hat of the good guy, just waiting to be unleashed against the criminal element of Alabama; not the black hat of my brothers and sisters in the criminal defense bar, friends and beer buddies often; adversaries always and in all ways.

Since I've already given you a taste of Port City politics and what passed for justice in that arena, I might as well give you a full lick of the cone of good old garden variety corruption and how it manifested itself in Mobile on a fairly regular basis, particularly in the early and mid 1980s. The biggest story coming out of Mobile during this period of years was the corruption in government which seemed to ooze from the very cracks in the sidewalk. And the biggest manifestation of that corruption was the ongoing scam at the Mobile Civic Auditorium.

By the time that I was officially on the payroll at the Mobile DA's Office, Galanos had managed, albeit clumsily and almost accidentally, but always with the best of intentions and purest of motives, to pass enough ammunition to the enemy to accelerate the demise of the already rapidly sinking USS District Attorney. I began to wonder why I had left the relative comfort and security of Columbiana for the socially inbred corruption of Mobile.

COOKING THE BOOKS – MOBILE STYLE

THE LONG-TIME SCANDAL OF an on-going scam at the City Auditorium went back at least for several years, well back into the '70s, when a character named Buddy Clewis was the manager of the Auditorium. The scam that he ran while he was the manager involved "cooking the books" or at least maintaining two sets of books. One set was for public consumption that always showed a "legitimate" loss, attributable to what were said to be the rising costs of talent, concessions, etc. The second set reflected all legitimate costs in addition to the skim, that was split up in several ways, none of which were legal. And the beauty of the operation was that the city of Mobile financed the operations costs – not to mention the original construction costs – and the taxpayers were the ones who got soaked in a river of red ink.

Clewis was indicted and tried on one count of several that were issued by way of grand jury indictment. He was found not guilty by the jury in a somewhat curious prosecution in which, according to a number of seasoned observers, the State dropped the ball in what should have resulted in Clewis's conviction. After the acquittal, several remaining counts were dismissed by the State in as much as the State maintained that it had tried the strongest count, and that further prosecutions likely would have the same result.

The prosecutor was hard-charging Charley Graddick, who later was elected Alabama Attorney General, and who ran for governor in 1986, but had the Democratic Nomination stripped from him by the United States Court of Appeals of the Eleventh Circuit and later by a group of five Democrats from the State Democratic Executive Committee. Each of the two bodies said essentially that Graddick won the Democratic Primary by not playing fair. And thus, Bill Baxley, favorite son of the political "in" group, was designated the Democratic nominee for governor by the Democratic Executive Committee, the "gang of five."

That action, taken during the summer of 1986, caused the biggest upheaval in Alabama politics since Reconstruction. The result was the state's electing Guy Hunt, a Probate Judge and Amway salesman from Cullman County, as its first Republican Governor of the twentieth century. And things have never been the same in a state where politics is as big, or bigger, than high school and college football. Graddick is now a circuit judge in Mobile County. Sometimes life takes strange turns — more often than not, it seems, in Mobile County.

But the unraveling of all this corruption began with one person who was curious enough to wonder why the auditorium was losing all the money that the local fish wrapper, The Mobile *Press Register,* reported that it lost. That person was Bill Steele, classmate of mine and the individual most responsible for paving the way for me to imitate Daniel and walk right in amongst the lions. Actually, lions have some integrity and will eat you only if they're hungry. A den of vipers is closer to what I found waiting for me in Mobile.

"Stainless" Steele is now a United States district court judge, and he won that black robe the old-fashioned way — he earned it. Bill's wife Linda also achieved heroine status in her capacity as an auditor for the city of Mobile. If you're going to run a crooked operation, don't ever hire an honest auditor for the organization, particularly one who is married to an honest and curious prosecutor. Ultimately, the auditorium case resulted in numerous federal and state prosecutions and in spin-off cases which developed from the original investigation. Put another way, every time a state or federal prosecutor kicked over a rock to kill the snake that tried to hide under it, two more slithered out.

During the year 1982, and continuing on into 1983, Bill Steele noticed several articles in the *Press Register*, which reported continuing losses at the Mobile Civic Auditorium, a public facility financed and operated with public funds. Sometime in the spring of that year, Bill's wife Linda, an accountant with the City of Mobile, was bothered by a check for a nominal amount of money which came from the City Auditorium account. She couldn't reconcile it, and couldn't find anybody in the finance department who could or would explain it to her satisfaction. She took the check home to show to Bill, and it immediately raised his suspicions, particularly in light of his earlier curiosity about the continuing losses at the City Auditorium._

That element of curiosity combined with a good prosecutor's suspicions led to the opening of the second, and more successful, "Auditorium Investigation." That investigation, coupled with an already existing federal probe of corruption in the state court system of Mobile County, led to probably the longest series of investigations and prosecutions of corruption – in one form or another – in the history of Mobile County.

Before it was over several years down the road, numerous elected officials, judges and all but invisible power brokers, ended up serving lengthy sentences in either state or federal prison. Those prosecutions probably created a cleaner Mobile for at least a good five years before it was back to its wicked ways. But bad habits are hard to break, particularly those born of greed and a love of power, regardless of how attained and kept.

Ultimately, most of the beneficiaries of the corruption found themselves out of jobs and new residents of any of a number of federal and state correction facilities. But getting the ammunition to put them there became almost too big and tough an obstacle to overcome. But the bigger question was the identity of the "he coon" of the whole crooked operation – and I don't limit the corruption to just the chicanery at the auditorium. There was more, much more, which emerged in the coming years.

The answer became known more than a decade after I left Mobile with the separate federal prosecutions of Lee Jackson and the Godfather himself, Ellis McDonald. Before it was over, Jackson had been indicted for capital murder, with charges being dismissed in mid-trial, notwithstanding the fact that he was guilty as hell. A man named Doughty and his wife were executed in the kitchen of their own house, the motive never being revealed except that logically the murders were related to the corruption in that Mr. Doughty worked for one of the businesses which benefited directly from one aspect of the on going political corruption. Mrs. Doughty was killed simply because she had the misfortune of being present when her husband was loosed from the burdens of continuing to live.

But Chris made what many of us believe was a hasty and ill-considered decision to move the court to dismiss charges upon discovering that his star witness had committed perjury in giving testimony that totally exculpated himself in the conspiracy. Chris, to his credit, realized after the defendant's attorney had cross-examined Dicky Lane King that King had lied on the witness stand when he denied receiving money for supplying the gun to the two hired hit men. He truthfully testified that Jackson hired him to find two hit men and to supply them with the murder weapon, but he lied when he denied that he had been paid to serve as the middle man. And on re-direct examination the next day, after Chris had browbeaten in his office him into admitting that he lied, he corrected his perjured testimony.

However, Chris, in absolute good faith, decided not to proceed based on King's original perjured testimony. In all likelihood, the jury still would have convicted Jackson. My hindsight, just like everyone else's, is always twenty-twenty. The circumstances of the case were labyrinthine, but not so difficult to hinder a future jury to convict one of the two hit men. The second was acquitted, a verdict which shocked most observers of the trial. But Lee Jackson was indicted and convicted in federal court for violating the Racketeer Influenced and Corrupt Organization (RICO) statute for committing acts possibly unrelated to the murders of the Doughtys.

Trying to tie together all of the pieces of that RICO charge together is more than a daunting task; it's damned near impossible in a lengthy and protracted investigation, much less a truncated version of that factually and legally complex case recounted in a few pages of a book. But state and federal authorities, working in concert with each other, managed to make corruption in the Port City a much riskier business than it had been for much of its history. everal educated leaps of faith must be made in order to connect the dots in some fashion which begins to make sense

All of which brings us back to the *second* Auditorium investigation. During the spring and summer of 1983, prior to my arrival in LA (Lower Alabama) in October, as the second investigation was heating up, so also were the temperatures of many of the power brokers who ran the city. When D.A.'s investigators began interviewing promoters, talent and facilities managers all over the South and Southwest, the shape and size of the corruption began to become manifest to even the average Joe and Jane on the street. The investigation attracted the interest not only of John & Jane Q. Public, but also that of anyone who had a vested interest in the *status quo ante* (pre-investigation) of politics and business in Mobile. If it had not attracted such official and unofficial interest, the gravy train almost certainly would have kept on running and some VIPs would never have ended up the state or federal big house.

Over the course of that hot and humid summer, the investigation simmered and then began to boil. And thus it came to be that in early November of 1983, grand jury subpoenas were issued and the doo-doo intersected the rotary blades. Gary Greenough, the most visible and powerful member of the troika which ruled the city of Mobile under its old system of dividing the power and authority among a three member commission, began to squirm, although a full-scale meltdown was still in the offing.

SIDETRACKED BY PURSUING THE PURSUER – THE DISTRICT ATTORNEY HIMSELF

BUT PRIOR TO THE issuing of the subpoenas, which really turned up the heat, a series of events took place which would challenge the imagination of the most drug addled screen writers in Hollywood to reduce to a story line and script. We now backtrack to early September of 1983 and the notorious "Galanos DUI Incident". Chris was divorced at the time, and his former wife had contacted him about some incident involving their young daughter.

The "emergency" was greatly overestimated, but Chris's mercurial personality and his initial concern for his daughter caused him to panic as he was attempting to drive to his former wife's house as quickly as possible. Quite by happenstance he saw a police car with a uniformed officer, seemingly an act of providence, but which proved to be anything but the hand of God at work. It prompted Chris to pull next to the squad car and ask the officer for an escort to his destination. Upon arrival, he jumped out of his car and ran up to the squad car to thank the man in blue. And thus began one of the strangest series of incidents ever to occur in Mobile's checkered political and legal history.

It seems that the officer had a rather checkered history of his own, and rumor had it that he was somehow tied in with the power structure being attacked by Galanos. Regardless of rumor, it became apparent that he was out to get Galanos one way or another. When the District Attorney approached the squad car to extend his thanks, the officer ordered him to sit in the back of the car because he was "drunk." Chris was not charged with any offense, but the cop ordered him to sit in the back of the patrol car until the officer's superiors arrived at the scene and prevailed upon reason, common sense, the law and the facts to persuade the patrol officer to release Galanos. And there the matter would have ended but for Galanos's penchant for shooting himself in the foot.

But Chris was never known for his ability to leave well enough alone. And so the next day he marched straight to the offices of the Mobile *Press Register* and informed an all ears reporter that on the previous evening he had been held prisoner for two hours in the back of a squad car on a trumped up DUI stop. I say trumped up because Galanos was not a drinker, although he had a bad Dexedrine habit. Chris had been taking the little "kick starters" for some period of time by virtue of one or more legal prescriptions, and it was generally a known fact in the legal community.

Problem was that he likely was obtaining the Dexedrine from more than one source, and had developed a dependency for the drug. Given the hours that he worked and his compulsion to stay so damned busy that he could outwork the bad guys, his overuse of the drug was hardly surprising. Until the auditorium investigation began, however, nobody much seemed to care whether Chris was using too many of his "mother's little helpers" to work the number of hours that he put in at the office. Once that rock was kicked over, and the snakes began slithering out, interest in "helping" poor Chris took off like a Roman candle on the Fourth of July.

But his relating of the previous night's events to the members of the fifth estate proved to be a near fatal mistake for his career. The next day's paper carried a front page story about Galanos's claims that he had been held "prisoner" in the back of a squad car for about two hours before being released. And that particular misstep gave the powers of darkness all the excuse they needed to "investigate" the particulars of Galanos's alleged driving under the influence of "something" and his being "held captive" for two hours in the back seat of the squad car. At the same time, it was no secret that the prospects of a full scale Grand Jury investigation of the hinky financial happenings at the City Auditorium had more than a few individuals in the power structure losing sleep at night.

Within approximately ten days, Robert Hodnette, presiding Circuit Judge and self-appointed person of power and influence, as well as protector of the status quo in Mobile, had convened a special grand jury with the sole charge of investigating the allegation that the District Attorney had been held against his will in the back of the squad car. During the course of the grand jury inquiry, somehow, thanks to Judge Hodnette, their charge came to include Galanos's supposed driving under the influence on the night of the sixth of September. And thus began the unfolding of a page in the political and judicial history of Mobile County that was better suited as a vehicle for either the Marx brothers or the Three Stooges.

The presiding judge himself was a fat, red-faced bully with a loud voice and a small brain. His stock-in-trade was coming up to an unsuspecting lawyer in the courthouse hallway, blasting him about some matter that should have been handled in the courtroom, and then turning and walking away before the poor lawyer could even think of a response, much less articulate it. He died several years ago, and I was taught not to speak ill of the dead. However, about the only good things I can say about the old coot are that he was a veteran, European theater, of World War II, and that he wasn't corrupt – at least not to the extent of being "on the take." Doing favors for friends and engaging in more than a little judicial "home cookin'" were altogether another matter.

But, I digress. The circus in the courthouse with Judge Hodnette as the ringmaster continued in mid-September with his convening a special grand jury to investigate the incident that occurred in early September. The honorable Judge Hodnette appointed one of his courthouse cronies, an otherwise undistinguished attorney named John Coleman, to head up the inquisition. Coleman spent the better part of a week drinking coffee and schmoozing with other courthouse cronies, occasionally calling a witness to testify before the grand jury.

But for the fact that Galanos himself, in his inimitable fashion of shooting himself in the foot when the Mongols were at the gates, had provided a sworn affidavit to the world at large that he had taken two Dexedrine capsules on the day in question, there would have been absolutely no evidence of any wrongdoing on his part, and even the substance of his admission would likely have been inadmissible if the court hearing that "evidence" had ruled in accord with the law and the applicable *rules* of evidence, and not on what a given judge thought those rules *should* have been.

But because of a "feeling" that a police officer with a very checkered past had, that Galanos *must* have been under the influence of *something*, or he wouldn't have been so excited, not only could that admission be used against Chris in any subsequent trial, but that all sorts of otherwise inadmissible evidence could be offered by the State in proving its case. That officer's conclusion, even if he were to be believed, in and of itself revealed that he knew next to nothing about the virtually always excitable Greek.

After about a week of coffee drinking and posturing in the courthouse hallways for the benefit of all who would look at him, Coleman presented a proposed indictment of Galanos for driving under the influence of Dexedrine. The Grand Jury returned a true bill of indictment, and Galanos's claims of "unlawful imprisonment" were quickly brushed aside if they had ever even been considered by that deliberative body of citizens. And Coleman, for his back breaking work with the grand jury, was enriched by the members of the County Commission to the tune of $25,000 of the taxpayer's money. That figure is not a misprint; the *Press Register* ran a photo copy of the check on the front page of the paper.

How the County Commissioners arrived at that rather munificent fee for Mr. Coleman's "expertise" with grand juries, as well as his crushing work load before them, was anybody's guess. However, those of us with just a very brief overview of the inner workings of government in the Independent Republic of Mobile could not be blamed for questioning why those members of the Commission thought that the indictment of the unpredictable, but not for sale, District Attorney could be worth that kind of money. But that was just the fee for doing "bid'ness" in Mobile. If you were on the "right" side, that is the side that used taxpayer funds to reward their friends, you could live quite comfortably while never having to break a sweat in doing your appointed chores.

Could it be that the power structure found it to their distinct disadvantage to have Chris Galanos continue to be the one elected official in the county who had the power and authority to throw a monkey wrench into the machinery of the genteel corruption that was a way of life in the Port City? And who was not only incorruptible himself, but also gutsy enough to throw that monkey wrench? Call me cynical, but I thought that to be the case. Fortunately, I was not alone in my estimation of why things operated in such a fashion in the Kingdom of Mobile. The federal government began to realize that the city and county of Mobile is known in the military as a "target-rich environment".

A Buffoon on the Bench and on the Take

While the auditorium investigation and the attempt to run Galanos out of office were ongoing, the feds were preparing a case for trial that, in my estimation, blew the doors off many of Mobile's inner sanctums of corruption and "deal cutting" by the good old boys and a few good old girls. For a considerable length of time in at least 1982 or 1983, Mobile Circuit Court Judge Elwood Hogan had engaged in the kind of zany and bizarre behavior that normally is rejected by Hollywood script writers as being too absurd to be accepted by movie patrons as anything even remotely resembling reality.

He would leave jurors in the box for an hour or two, cooling their heels while he took care of "other matters" in his office. On at least one occasion, he was gone for such an inordinate amount of time that the prosecutor went to Hogan's locked door and began trying to summon him to the bench before his antics instigated a juror revolt. After considerable banging on his door by the assistant district attorney, Judge Hogan, panting heavily, red-faced and disheveled, cracked open the door just wide enough to tell the prosecutor that he would be out in a few minutes, and also just wide enough for the prosecutor to see a similarly disheveled woman on Hogan's "casting couch." To say that he was an embarrassment to the general public, his brother judges and an overwhelming number of members of the Mobile Bar Association is to grossly understate the magnitude of his buffoonery.

He also had caught the attention of deputy prosecutors in the District Attorney's Office, as well as more than a few state probation officers with his rather imaginative rulings from the bench and, more particularly, his sentencing policies which seemed to have more than a casual relationship with which attorney represented which defendant and which defendant had the financial resources to obtain "justice." Prosecutors and probation officers alike began making "book" on the less than honorable Judge Elwood Hogan.

Also, he had proved to be such an embarrassment to the entire Bar Association, there sprang a concerted effort to defeat him in an election where incumbent judges rarely are challenged. Ted McDermott handily defeated him. And if Hogan hadn't been so greedy, he might have avoided the federal joint. But once you get used to being on the take, it's worse than trying to eat one salted peanut – you just have to keep going back for more. And poor, avaricious Elwood Hogan just couldn't resist inserting his sticky, grubby and chubby paw into the jar of forbidden cookies just one last time. And that jar of cookies was a doper named Lester Pugh.

It seems that Pugh had paid Hogan to give him probation for pleading guilty to possessing with the intent to distribute a fairly substantial amount of cocaine. The sentencing was carried out per the agreement, after Hogan's electoral defeat, but just before the expiration of his term. The stench from the sentencing permeated the courthouse and even drifted down to the offices of the FBI. Elwood either was too stupid – a real possibility – or too arrogant to realize that people were watching. But what the hell; bribery is very difficult to prove unless either the person paying the bribe or the one receiving it, runs his mouth about what went on in the dark corridors of corruption alley, which is just really part of the fabric of business and politics.

However, Hogan's stupidity and arrogance reached heretofore uncharted territory even for Mobile, Alabama. Because approximately two or three weeks after the big payoff, Hogan and Pugh were sighted, and photographed, I believe, on a gambling junket to Las Vegas by several Special Agents of the FBI who had been tipped off to keep a watchful eye on Hogan. And if memory serves me correctly, Pugh picked up the tab for Hogan. See what I mean about new standards for stupidity and arrogance being established by Hogan?

By this time, of course, the former judge's machinations were no longer a source of impetus for running him out of office; he needed to be run into the federal big house. He had committed the unpardonable sin of tainting and embarrassing the entire Mobile County judiciary, not to mention bringing serious disrepute and dishonor on the very integrity of the system itself. And for this breach of the belief in a fair-minded judiciary, regardless of how chimerical that belief might be, there must be a blood sacrifice.

But proving that money changed hands appeared to be a nearly insoluble problem. Everyone in law enforcement knows what is going on, but the dry rot is behind a protective shield of silence. Barring Hogan or Pugh bragging about the deal to an FBI undercover wearing a wire and a transmitter which would send out over the air waves any on-going conversation which would be recorded by an agent at another location who was also listening to the conversation in real time, the two likely would skate off into the sunset with smug looks at having beaten the system.

Sometimes, however, life takes strange and unexpected twists and turns. Elwood Hogan had grossly underestimated the reaction of the law enforcement and judicial communities. In an act of supreme irony, the tables were turned, and Hogan was caught with his robes off, his shorts down and his hand still reflexively clenching all of the bribes that he had taken as a sitting judge. Bob Hodnette, presiding judge and living symbol of Mobile's judiciary, did the right thing and ordered Pugh to be resentenced.

But this time, the fix definitely wasn't in and Pugh took a fifteen year hit and no probation. Pugh was out his money with nothing to show for it. In other words, his bribe money went down the tubes as he was headed for the "big house." It just wasn't fair, and Lester felt used and abused. Being a big believer in the credo that a man's word is his bond, Lester Pugh wanted what lawyers call *specific performance* on the contract. He complained to his lawyer, who was not in on the bribery, and they went to – you guessed it – the FBI. As they say, he spilled his guts to the Feds, who already were investigating Hogan.

Pugh's righteous indignation at actually being sentenced to prison for having sold a few ounces of cocaine, particularly when he felt that his bribe of Hogan was just another means of conducting his business, resulted in his giving evidence about the biggest conspiracy to "fix" cases ever to stain the judiciary in Alabama. As an added bonus, Pugh gave up several other courthouse rats who wanted their share of free cheese.

What amounted to a rather sizable conspiracy to buy and sell justice was revealed by Pugh to the Feds, and was the impetus for the Federal Grand Jury indicting more than a handful of these criminal members of the judiciary and its ancillary prosecutive – at least a wanna' be member of the prosecutive arm – and surety divisions. One of these vermin named was a lawyer named Willis Holloway, "the wanna' be," who had run against Galanos in the recent election and had come within 1,000 votes of unseating him as District Attorney. There were at least two bail bondsmen, Dodson Fail and Billy Broadus, and a district court judge who handled misdemeanors and preliminary hearings on felony offenses, Jimmy Sullivan.

Had it not been for Hogan's arrogance and stupidity, as well as for Holloway's narrow loss to Galanos, the crooks would have owned the courthouse – lock, stock, tomahawk and gavel. Think about it: with the exception of somebody in the clerk's office to play games with the files, the bad guys would have a crook in virtually every key position in the courthouse. The bondsmen handled negotiations with the defendants; Judge Sullivan handled misdemeanors and preliminary hearings; any cases that reached Hogan were handled by him; and Willis Holloway, had he been elected, could have personally handled all plea agreements. Everyone, except justice and the general public would have made out like bandits.

But Hogan pushed the envelope too far, and the federal indictments rolled down like water from a cleansing mountain spring.

JEFF SESSIONS TO THE RESCUE

IN FEBRUARY OF 1984, after a couple of the ne'er do wells had pled guilty and "flipped" on the others, proving again the old maxim that there is no honor among thieves, a federal jury convicted every one of the remaining crooks on every count in the indictment.

The chief prosecutor was an apple-cheeked and near anonymous young United States Attorney named Jefferson Beauregard Sessions. He later was nominated to be a United States federal district court judge, but was slandered at his confirmation hearing by the likes of

Teddy Kennedy and his ilk on the Senate Judiciary Committee, and never received a straight up or down vote by the full Senate. Jeff got the last laugh, however, when he later successfully ran for the United States Senate, and is now a member of the very Judiciary Committee which put the knife in his back. Ted Kennedy, in his sober moments, must believe that God is dead. Senator Sessions, however, knows that there is a God, and that He has an absolutely divine sense of humor.

The convictions of the courthouse gang breathed new hope into the citizens of Mobile County. For the first time in years, perhaps decades, the citizenry could see light where there had been only the darkness of corruption. People with knowledge of wrong doing emerged from their bunkers and began telling their stories to federal agents, DA's investigators and the Mobile *Press Register*. And all of this activity was occurring as the District Attorney's investigation of the city auditorium continued apace. Of course, the efforts to get Galanos removed from office were ongoing, and some scary things happened before the federal trial of the state court judges and their stooges.

THE DAY-TO-DAY BUSINESS OF WEEDING THE GARDEN

AND SO WE RETURN to the events of the fall of 1983. Notwithstanding the indictment of Galanos for driving under the influence of Dexedrine, business continued in the D.A.'s office at its usual frantic pace. Street crime of the garden variety – drugs, murders, burglaries, robberies, et.al. continued unabated, generating more work for the guardians of the gate separating the civilized folks from the Mongol hordes. Pleas were taken and trials were conducted at lightning speed. Our office tried more cases with fewer prosecutors than any other circuit in the state, including Jefferson County, home of Birmingham and Bessemer.

Murders normally could be divided into two camps by way of circumstance, social standing of the players, and a direct corollary of the first two – whether the public at large gave a tinker's damn about either the "victim" or the perpetrator. Anybody who had a social register listing at least two years in a row, be he "vic" or "perp," automatically caught the attention of the literate public. Literate in the sense that they read more than the daily installment of "Doonesbury" in the local rag. The second category of killin' was normally what we irreverently referred to as a "dude–icide". That's a homicide wherein one dude ices another, be it by firearm, knife, bare hands or something really exotic and imaginative like a Molotov cocktail.

Dude-icides were normally black on black, but certainly were not limited by race. The deciding factor generally was social standing or place of residence in the community. For example, most of the dude-icides occurred in locations such as Davis Avenue, while virtually all of the murders of a higher social order, those few that did occur, took place in places like Spring Hill, one of Old Mobile's tonier neighborhoods, or at least in socially similar locales. But our defendants represented the apotheosis of diversity. Black, white, brown, blue collar, white collar, young and old they came. And we gleefully prosecuted them all, without regard to race, creed, color or sexual preference. Our office was a veritable study in brotherhood, in a rather perverse way.

It was not at all unusual for one of our prosecutors to try two or even three cases in a week. And we had some top of the line litigators such as Tom Harrison, Don Beebe, Gloria Bedwell, Joe Thetford, Chris Hargett, Bill Steele and Lloyd Copeland, as well as the DA himself, Chris Galanos. I was an eager neophyte myself, but was tossed into the fire and learned quickly. After the first of the year we had a new prosecutor join the office, Teresa Tanner, who became a superstar in her own right. She later married and joined the DA's office in Birmingham as Teresa Pulliam. I had the pleasure of working with Teresa in both circuits.

In addition to our excellent team of prosecutors, we also had the best investigative staff in the state, headed by the best investigator I ever worked with, Bob Eddy. I learned so much from Bob about conducting proper investigations, coordinating case preparation with the investigator, the importance of detail and literally scores of other matters related to criminal investigations and prosecution that I could spend days talking about what I learned from him. If I became a very good prosecutor I can thank numerous individuals for helping me get there. But Bob Eddy would be at the top of the list, hands down.

BACK TO THE EMBATTLED DISTRICT ATTORNEY AND THE "MIDNIGHT MOVE" OF THE AUDITORIUM FILES

BUT AS GOOD, COLLECTIVELY and individually, as our prosecutors were, we all were concerned with "the forces of darkness" eagerly and relentlessly at work to get our boss out of office. And, while we all may have been running high on the paranoia index, that reading did not even slightly affect the reality that a number of powerful people would have slept much easier with Galanos out of office and selling real estate in Gulf Shores.

The real fear was that the underlying reason for the prosecution on the DUI charge was not that Chris would be convicted of the offense. There was no evidence of such an offense except Chris's admission that he had taken two Dexedrine capsules on the morning of the incident. But the discovery process, aided by a most unusual pre-trial ruling from the designated trial judge, likely would yield evidence of *habitual* use of the substance. That fact alone could be used to impeach him and remove him from office. No conviction of the underlying DUI case would even be required. And the instrument of that anticipated attempt at impeachment was one Charles Graddick, Attorney General of Alabama, and immediate predecessor of Chris Galanos as District Attorney of Mobile County.

Graddick was such an exaggeration of a bad guy that he actually came off as a caricature, or even as a cartoon of one. Snidely Whiplash of <u>Rocky and Bullwinkle</u> fame immediately comes to mind. But his actions were nothing like those of the clumsy antics of Wile E. Coyote of *Roadrunner* fame. Formerly a deputy district attorney in Mobile, he rose to position of District Attorney of Mobile County and ultimately was elected Attorney General of Alabama, largely on the strength of his televised advertisement to "Fry 'Em 'Till Their Eyeballs Pop Out!" in enforcing the state's death penalty. Ironically, Graddick, in all of his various incarnations as a prosecutor, succeeded in having more death penalty sentences reversed by appellate courts than probably any other Alabama prosecutor, many, if not most, being reversed for improper argument.

Interestingly, after his ill fated run for governor in 1986, followed by several years private practice in Montgomery, he returned to Mobile and now serves as a circuit judge. Who knows what the future holds for both Judge Graddick and the people of Mobile County with "Electric Chair" Charley on the bench? Except that now, due to a change in Alabama law, he may become known as "Lethal Injection" Charley, or simply as the "Drip."

But back when he was elected Attorney General, in 1978 I believe, he fashioned himself as a kingmaker as well as an elected official. Someone would have to be appointed to serve the remainder of Graddick's term until the next general election. Graddick apparently assumed that the new Governor, Fob James, would accommodate Charley by appointing one of his own people, probably Don Valeska. And thus, Charley would find it much easier to keep his finger on the pulse of the old homestead as well as to have his chosen one even more beholden to him. But James, after being inaugurated, threw a monkey wrench into the deal. A Greek monkey wrench named Galanos.

And the law books hit the fan when Galanos walked into his office his first day on the job. One tip of the hat that I'll give to Charley is that he somehow managed to inspire loyalty from most of his troops. My understanding is that many of them, support staff included, walked out the door when Chris walked in on that fateful first day. You see, Graddick considered his office to be his personal fiefdom, and was of the opinion that the new governor should see it that way also. I guess that Fob James must have missed that memo. Thus, bad blood existed from the get go between Graddick and Galanos. And subsequent events in the fall of 1983 did nothing to heal Graddick's wounded pride and sense of proprietorship in his home county.

The table was set for any opportunity that might present itself to Charley to regain control of the DA's Office by somehow ridding it of Chris and having his own man step into the job. The thinking was that if Galanos embarrassed himself sufficiently, he could somehow be removed from office and Fob James would simply wash his hands of the whole sordid affair, leaving it to Graddick to hand-pick his own man. Of course, the foregoing scenario is merely speculation, but every person in our office believed it to be an accurate analysis of future events.

The first thing that "Chargin'" Charley did was to appoint a special prosecutor, otherwise known as a Special Assistant Attorney General. Such appointments of attorneys in private practice are made traditionally by Attorneys General either because their office has a conflict of interest, a rare occurrence, or as a political plum ($) given to reward a friend or political supporter of the Attorney General. I didn't know much about Ira DeMent at the time, but following the special grand jury's indictment of Galanos, I made it my business to find out whatever I could about the man.

A classmate of mine who did some legal research for DeMent during our third year in law school, described him to me as someone having the legal acumen of a perpetual guardian *ad litem*. All of which is to say he wasn't the brightest pup in the litter. But when your jaws have a death grip on the biggest tit available – the coffers of the state treasury in this instance – you don't have to be the second coming of Perry Mason in order to pay your bar tab. Whether he was a friend or political supporter of Graddick, I don't know; I just know that anyone in Graddick's office could try a driving under the influence case. But that would be a salaried employee and not a practicing attorney who could bill the state for every hour, in court and out of court, "working" on the post-indictment investigation and trial. Of course, the man today sits as a Federal district court judge. He must have done a hell of a job with that DUI prosecution.

What he *did* do well was to strut around like a peacock at the Riverview Plaza Hotel, drink in hand, and be impressed with his own exaggerated sense of self importance. He also had two investigators assigned to him from Graddick's office, and their main purpose in being in Mobile seemed to be functioning as shadows for Galanos wherever he traveled. Besides strutting around like a little banty rooster, DeMent filed a few motions with the Court, one of which was the key to the political future of Chris Galanos. The substance of that motion was to request that the records of Galanos's prescriptions for Dexedrine be admitted as evidence at trial to prove that Chris was under the influence of that drug when driving on the night in question.

Interestingly, Graddick appointed Dement on November 4, 1983, the same date that Mr. Galanos was composing a list of witnesses who would be called to appear before the Investigatory Grand Jury then scheduled to convene on November 7, three days later. Also occurring on November 4, and of particular interest in the efforts being exerted to stop the investigation in its tracks, City Commissioner Gary Greenough was served a subpoena summoning him to appear before the Grand Jury. And that's when it really hit the fan. Literally within minutes of the subpoena being served on Greenough, Chief Deputy District Attorney Tom Harrison was commanded to appear before "King Bob" Hodnette in chambers. There, Harrison was told by Hodnette that he, Judge Hodnette, had cancelled the upcoming grand jury, thus effectively putting a halt to the auditorium investigation.

A judge from Montgomery was imported to preside over the proceedings of the earlier Grand Jury which returned the indictment charging Chris with DUI. To the amazement of most individuals familiar with the rules of evidence, he granted the prosecution's request as to the medical records for one year prior to the driving incident. The ruling was tantamount to the admission of a person's bar bills for a year prior to an allegation of drunk driving. No court with which I am familiar would admit such "evidence."

But if the purpose of the motion was merely to ensure the publication of those records in a public forum, said publication to be used to prove that someone had an addiction to prescription drugs, an impeachable offense under the Constitution of Alabama, then such a ruling made perfect sense. Whether that scenario was grounded in fact is mere speculation, but legally and politically, it seemed to those of us in the D.A.'s office the only explanation for such a bizarre set of circumstances and legal rulings.

And from that point, it seemed to us that Mr. Graddick would exercise his authority to continue (or not) the ongoing investigation of corruption at the Mobile City Auditorium, and the investigation would be sucked into a black hole, never to emerge in the form of criminal indictments. Call it group paranoia or whatever else you want to label the mind set of virtually everyone in the District Attorney's office that fall, but we all breathed a sigh of relief when agents of the FBI, led by now deceased Special Agent Moss Stack, assisted Bill Steele and Tom Harrison, literally under cover of darkness one night after work, in moving the investigatory files to federal custody, thus thwarting any possible attempt by state authorities to kill the investigation. The actual removal of the files occurred on November 8, 1983.

And while all of these proceedings were ongoing, Mr. DeMent continued the circus in which the fast approaching Galanos trial was the main attraction. Chris was represented by Billy Kimbrough, former United States Attorney, and notable courtroom bulldog. Hardly a person to be intimidated or out-lawyered by the likes of Charley Graddick or Ira DeMent. But Graddick insisted on dictating the terms of a proposed plea agreement to Ira DeMent, over the telephone at that, and the specifics were so onerous as to all but guarantee a trial. Those terms were that Chris plead guilty to the DUI charge and take an indefinite leave of absence from the D.A.'s office, the length of the leave to be determined by Graddick, and a stay at a rehabilitation center to be chosen by Graddick.

And sure enough; on the morning of the trial, a jury was struck and in the box when the forces of darkness blinked and the case was settled in a fashion that could only be described as a TKO (technical knock-out) by Galanos and Kimbrough over Graddick and his now thoroughly intimidated surrogate, Ira DeMent. The charges were dismissed with prejudice – they could never be revived – and Galanos agreed to take a one month leave of absence and check into a rehabilitation center of his own choosing.

Several matters need to be discussed briefly before this matter is put to bed. First, it is apparent that Chris Galanos had developed a dependency on the prescription drug Dexedrine, and that he had more than one prescription for the drug which could be filled at several pharmacies. Second, that his dependency, while not widely known by the general public, was subject to some discussion within the legal community. Third, Chris was not a drinker, and certainly had not been drinking on the occasion when he was confronted by the Mobile police officer on the occasion when he got out of his car to thank the officer for the escort to the house of his former wife and mother of his child. Fourth, that the officer had quite a checkered past and was rumored to be at the beck and call of Gary Greenough, the commissioner in charge of the city auditorium. Fifth, that evening he was not charged with any violation, certainly not with being under the influence of any substance.

Finally, ask yourself this question: *Cui bono*? Who would benefit by a public revelation that Chris Galanos, District Attorney of Mobile County, was dependent on Dexedrine, and thus would be subject to the possibility of impeachment from office under the State Constitution for being a habitual drug abuser? I rest my case.

As much as I detested Charley Graddick, however, for what I and many others perceived during the 80's as his total lack of character and integrity, fairness demands that I rethink some of my bad feelings about the man. He now is a circuit court judge in Mobile and, apparently has acquired some judicial temperament, as well as judicious behavior, along with his black robe. My rethinking of my attitude and feelings toward "Electric Chair Charley" remained unchanged until I had a conversation with Bill Steele about him in the writing of this book.

Bill told me that Charley had made a change for the good and that it seemed legitimate. Hearing that from anyone but Bill Steele would cause my personal BS meter to go off the chart. But coming from now United States District Judge Steele, whose opinion carries a lot of weight with me, it seems likely that our former Attorney General has undergone a genuine transformation of character. His mean spirit during a very mean-spirited time in Mobile may have been infused at this time in his life with the humanity and humility of a man who has reached a level of insight and understanding of his own frailties to which the rest of us can only aspire. If so, he may just prove himself to be an outstanding judge. One can only hope, but I have received similar reports from people whose judgment I trust. Thus, it seems likely that Judge Graddick has genuinely and legitimately changed for the better.

And thus, the great DUI controversy of 1983 came to a halt with a whimper and not the bang which so many had expected and predicted. But life continued in the DA's Office and corruption continued virtually unabated in Mobile County. Just another example of good being skin deep, but corruption running all the way to the marrow of the bone. Chris took a thirty day leave of absence and left Tom Harrison in charge of the office. And within six months after his return to the office, Chris had managed to plunge into hot water once again. But that episode can be put off for the moment.

The Klan Takes One on the Chin and into the Chair

During all of the excitement, intrigue and fear of the weeks preceding Chris's date with destiny, the daily work of the DA's Office continued without missing a beat or a docket call. And that included one of the most important and historically significant cases ever tried in the South – the capital murder case of Henry Hays, Ku Klux Klan member in good standing and killer of Michael Donald, a young black man who happened to be in the wrong place at the wrong time. Michael Donald was nineteen years old, and hadn't done anything bad to anyone, except to be born black and offend the sensibilities of the local chapter of the Klan by virtue of his skin color.

The members of that chapter of the KKK were angry because a black thug had murdered a white police officer in Birmingham after first robbing a downtown department store. Of course that city had its own legacy of mutual distrust and total segregation of the two races. The venue of the trial was moved to Mobile because of the extensive publicity in Birmingham.

The case was mistried three times before a jury finally convicted the defendant, Josephus Anderson, after the fourth and final trial. Interestingly, the prosecutor in all four trials was David Barber, my future boss in the first three trials, and my actual boss in the fourth. David would have tried that case either until he got a verdict or until the Alabama Supreme Court told him to stop. David was not particularly fond of cop killers. Hays and his Klan buddies literally lynched Michael Donald after the first or second mistrial in order to demonstrate white power. Unfortunately, all that they demonstrated was that there were still parts of the United States where a group of ignorant, hateful men could burn crosses and kill young men solely because of the color of their skin.

Chris had intended to try the case himself, but the timing of the plea agreement in the DUI case made it absolutely necessary for someone else to take on the Klan and its emissary, Henry Hays. Tom Harrison, pro that he was, picked up the case file about a week before trial, got up to speed, and tried it without breaking a sweat. The jury convicted Hays of capital murder, and Judge Braxton Kittrell sentenced him to death. Several years later, that sentence was carried out, and Henry Hays joined one or two other white men in the United States in the twentieth century to be executed for killing a black man.

Chris Steps in it Again

The year 1983 drew to a close, and in February of 1984, the corruption trial in federal court of the state judges and lawyers ended in total victory for the good guys. Concurrently, the auditorium investigation rolled on like a boulder down a hill, picking up plenty of moss on its journey, all the while just looking for someone to roll over and flatten. And that journey led directly to the thieves who had been looting the coffers of the Mobile Civic Auditorium for more than a decade.

But before that investigation came to fruition, I was cutting my prosecutorial teeth on the likes of Michael Otis Mitchell and other denizens of various sewers in Mobile County, and the crazy life in our little piece of hell continued unabated. Chris Galanos managed to be the target of a second Grand Jury investigation, this being one of the strangest chapters in a very strange judicial and political chapter of the long and sordid history of the Port City. And strangely enough, the federal case managed to save Chris from yet another tar baby that he had jumped into and embraced with gusto.

Sometime in the spring of 1984, Chris was at a party. Also there was his former wife Gwin, who also was the mother of their beloved child, Kristin. Enter the villain, David Nihart, local lawyer and disk jockey. I don't know whether he also did automotive body work and styled men's hair on the side, but he was still quite the Renaissance man. At some point during the evening's frivolities Nihart and Gwin absented themselves from the premises, followed not too much later by the jealous Greek himself, Chris Galanos.

Without enumerating the details of the unseemly activities that followed their arrival at David Nihart's house, the three soon were embroiled in a series of events so outlandish as to seem comical if they hadn't been so serious with so much at stake. Within but a few minutes, Nihart's nose began bleeding profusely where it had made contact with Chris's right fist. Chris called in the paramedics for Nihart, and the whole silly business would have remained a private matter between consenting adults, but for the fact that this was Mobile, and things happened in Mobile that were foreign to more civilized parts of the world.

Several weeks after the incident, which had remained private to that point, Galanos was visited by Nihart in his office who presented him with a choice: resign as District Attorney or be arrested for burglary in the first degree, a class A felony in the state of Alabama, carrying a penalty of ten years to life. Predictably, and justifiably, Chris threw him out of his office.

Nihart then went to a district court judge in a vain attempt to swear out a warrant charging Galanos with burglary in the first degree. Nihart alleged that Galanos broke into his house with the attempt to commit a crime, assault. Chris maintained that, although he broke several panes of glass in the French doors to Nihart's house when he kicked the doors, Nihart himself unlocked them and let him into the house. And Chris admitted punching Nihart's nose when he saw his former wife in the bedroom. The district court judge told Nihart, in effect, that he would issue a felony warrant for the incident described by the aggrieved victim when hell froze over. He did, however, tell Nihart that he would okay a warrant for a misdemeanor assault. Nihart left in a huff, *sans* warrant, and enlisted the aid of others with more clout than he possessed.

And thus, the summer of 1984 started with a bang, and fortunately ended with a whimper. But not before the Grand Inquisitor himself, Judge Robert Hodnett, convened a second special grand jury for the purpose of investigating the alleged "burglary" perpetrated by Galanos. Even Charley Graddick, sworn enemy of Galanos and anyone associated with him, had grown weary of the continuing circus in his home city. He still wanted Galanos out of office, but he certainly didn't need a repeat of the judicial follies of several months prior to the latest bit of tomfoolery taking place in Mobile. And so for this go-'round he skipped the political clowns and buffoons who had run the show in the fall of '83. And he sent in two of his best prosecutors who could not only spell *integrity*, but also lived it, John Gibbs and Ed Carnes. Carnes is now a federal appeals court judge in the Eleventh Circuit.

Judge Hodnette convened the special grand jury and the subpoenas went flying all over the courthouse, including those for every person – prosecutors to secretaries – who worked in the DA's Office, all for the purpose of finding out what we knew and when we knew it, about the bloody nose of Nihart and the broken panes of glass in the French doors. I must say that I was not amused nor in the best of moods when I was served my subpoena.

When I testified, I behaved like anything but a professional and a gentleman. Essentially I told the grand jury that this entire operation was a railroad job and that Bob Hodnette was the engineer driving the train. I think Gibbs and Carnes must have been more than a little nervous with this crazy man testifying. However, they took it in stride like the professionals they were and the grand jury did its job, indicting Chris for the misdemeanor charge of assault in the third degree. You may note that the charge returned by way of the grand jury's indictment was precisely the offense that the district court judge had said that he would okay weeks before the jugglers, plate balancers and elephant poop shovelers hit town.

While all of this nonsense was occurring, the FBI and the United States Attorney's Office continued their investigation of the city auditorium and the corruption associated with it. George Juzang, manager of the auditorium and David Gwin, the assistant manager, both had been indicted by the federal grand jury in Mobile for their engineering of the keeping of two sets of books, submitting phony ticket counts, and ripping off the city and the talent of their rightful shares of concessions sold at various events. Their trial was set for late summer.

The Friday before a jury was to be selected, they and their attorneys got dealt a joker that few saw coming, and folded their hand. In the parlance of the criminal justice system, they rolled over, cutting the best deal possible for themselves and "giving up" the bigger fish. And, in exchange for their cooperation, they had to be totally truthful about their knowledge of and/or/ participation in the dirty land deals, payoffs, kickbacks and other corruption going on at that time in the city and the county.

And some of those "fish" were about as big as anything swimming or sailing in Mobile Bay. Among them were the "Top Cat" himself, Gary Greenough, head of the troika that ruled Mobile from City Hall. Over the course of the next several years, numerous elected officials were prosecuted either by the state or by the federal government, and Mobile was cleaned up – at least for the next few years when a new crop of crooks was cultivated.

But Gwin and Juzang threw a wicked curve ball when they began cooperating. Each of them revealed that they had approached David Nihart with the assurance that if he pressed charges against Galanos in the now notorious "burglary" incident, they would see to it that he received a substantial portion of the city's legal business. Suffice it to say that the Attorney General, Charley Graddick, must have been grinding his teeth and wetting his bed when Jeff Sessions, then the United States Attorney for the Southern District of Alabama, called him and told him that his star witness against Galanos might have gotten his skirts a little muddy in his dealings with Gwin and Juzang. Reluctantly, and with a good deal of vitriol, Graddick dismissed the charge returned by the grand jury. "Mr. Lucky" (Galanos) dodged yet another bullet.

Ultimately, the series of investigations, state and federal, resulted in the successful prosecution several years thereafter of Mobile's very own Godfather – Ellis McDonald, the "he coon" himself – and owner of the local dog track, as well as an outside-the-law entrepreneur. He had a thumb in every pie, and never let the constraints of state or federal law slow him down. He called the shots in the Port City, and when he said *"Jump,"* most of the elected officials in the county inquired *"How high?"* on their way up.

The federal government finally found enough witnesses who weren't afraid to testify and enough documentary evidence existed to corroborate their testimony. McDonald was indicted and convicted of a federal RICO (Racketeer Influenced Corrupt Organization) violation sometime in the 1990s and his conviction ended an era of business and political chicanery in Mobile that all started with a "fubar" (fouled up beyond all repair) car stop of the District Attorney in September of 1983. But with his demise as the kingpin, Mobile became less of a haven for crime and more of a city of the Old South with aspirations of entering the twentieth century, if not the twenty-first.

JURIES, JERKS AND OTHER ASPECTS OF TRYING CASES IN MOBILE

PUT SIMPLY, JURIES METE out justice as they see it, and aren't necessarily constrained from or compelled to render their verdicts in strict accord with the law or the facts. Oh, they'll almost always have a reason for their verdict which can be squared often enough with the legal instructions given to them by the judge, and most of the time they even get it right. But sometimes a jury will return a verdict that causes a collective "huh?" This utterance of bewilderment and amazement can be heard throughout the courthouse and sometimes in a shot heard 'round the world. I give you Exhibit A for your consideration, O.J. Simpson.

Mike Rasmussen, one of the best prosecutors that I ever met, whom I had the pleasure of calling a colleague and friend during my tenure as a federal prosecutor, told me that he absolutely believed that no jury would ever convict a defendant unless they *wanted* to convict him. I always maintained that Mike was about ninety per cent correct, but that there were some juries that could, in effect, be *shamed* into convicting a person that they liked and didn't really want to convict. I had personally observed a jury on more than one occasion convict a defendant of the most serious charge available for their consideration when I know that they wanted a reason – any reason – to acquit or to find him guilty of some lesser offense than the most serious charged in the indictment.

I soon learned from personal experience in the courtrooms on the second floor of the old courthouse that if you were lucky enough to be a member of a FOMF, yet unlucky enough to be charged with a crime, your family status could be an affirmative defense in Mobile Circuit Court. Thus, not only did you enter the courtroom with the presumption of innocence, the State had the burden of proving your guilt beyond *all* doubt, not just reasonable doubt.

Additionally, you and your attorney were extended certain courtesies by the court not available to the general public and/or the prosecutor. For example, the Rules of Evidence sometimes were construed in a fashion that provided for a presumption against admissibility of evidence or testimony when offered by the prosecutor, and a presumption of admissibility when offered by the defendant. But, hey! Who ever said that it was going to be easy?

Such judicial practices are not limited to Mobile; they simply are exercised more frequently, egregiously and artfully there than in other jurisdictions. And if you don't learn to play by the rules of the only game in town very quickly after hitting the daily routine of pleas, trials, sentencings and such, you find yourself going down for the third time with no life jacket and the Coast Guard not in sight. Put another way, if you're going to fight city hall with any degree of success, you'd better remember who's paying the freight for the referee. And it isn't you.

Don't mistake that last sentiment as a not too thinly veiled suggestion that the judges in Mobile County and the "justice" that they dispensed was for sale. The only two gavel pounders in Mobile that I am aware of who were on the take, Jimmy Sullivan and Elwood Hogan, have already been discussed in these memoirs. As you know, both of those weasels were caught and convicted in federal court in February of 1984.

And there was a judge in Birmingham cut from the same bolt of cloth as these two and who was caught dirty several years later. "Mad Jack" Montgomery was as crazy as a run-over dog and as crooked as a card sharp in a New Orleans bawdy house, dealing off the bottom of the deck with his left hand while picking your pocket with his right one. But his story has been told before; thus, I will refrain from writing in detail about it.

I am merely saying that, with the exceptions of Hogan and Sullivan, the Mobile judiciary did little more than engage in a little home cookin' in the courtroom of a kind that every practicing trial lawyer throughout the country has experienced in his own jurisdiction. The judges in Mobile just seemed to be better at it than judges in other venues. Of course, the reality was that most of the judges, most of the time, were the impartial arbitrators that their black robes required them to be. But virtually every attorney, me included, vastly overstates any jurist's perceived bias against his case.

Of course, we prosecutors ourselves often were the beneficiaries of largesse from the bench. We just tended to disregard those occasions when computing the calculus of whether a given judge was "pro-prosecution" or "pro-defense" in his rulings. As I said, however, on some not totally rare instances, it really seemed that if the poor defendant wasn't connected to the "right" Mardi Gras Crewe, or a member of a FOMF, his chances of receiving favorable treatment in rulings from the bench were greatly reduced, and those of the prosecutor commensurately enhanced. And we, the representatives of the great state of Alabama, would grab the goodies dispensed by the figure in the black dress, the one holding the gavel and making the evidentiary decisions, and run like thieves in the night.

We would be giggling like school children who have managed to capture and scoop up spilled candy on Halloween night. Picture the scene after some clumsy old coot trying to help out his wife with the "trick or treaters," has dropped the plastic pumpkin filled with miniature Tootsie Rolls and candy corn. We prosecutors were the little urchins scooping up more than our fair share. And justice, of a sort, would be done.

Now that you have been dipped into the fetid muck of Mobile County politics and corruption, I'll give you a glimpse of how my education as a trial attorney sometimes hurt worse than an abscessed tooth about to explode. In the Circuit Court of Mobile County in the spring of 1984, when I was really beginning to feel cocky about my ability to try even the weakest of cases and still get a conviction, I prosecuted an absolutely guilty defendant in a domestic kidnapping case. Under Alabama law, kidnapping in the first degree has alternate definitions, including the holding of a person against his will with the intent to inflict serious bodily injury.

In this mini-drama, Dianne Nelson, the ex-wife, was held against her will at gunpoint for several hours, pistol-whipped by Archie, the ex-husband, and designated by him for execution. The sole reason that he was at her house at all was for the purpose of returning their infant son after his court-ordered visitation. As usual, he was about two hours late in returning the child. In tow with him was a drunken buddy who probably had nothing better to do on this particular day.

The child's mother was concerned that Archie might show up drunk and abusive. That type of behavior was typical of him, and he had the documented track record to prove it. She had already told her ten-year old son to go out the back window and head to the police station if Archie showed up in the anticipated foul mood and inebriated condition caused by hours of drinking whisky and beer and brooding about how life had been so unfair to him. Sure enough, Archie showed up in the anticipated condition with their less-than-two-year-old baby, a drunken friend, a loaded pistol in hand and a shotgun loaded for bear – or his wife – in his truck. Dianne saw what was about to occur and she hastily called the Saraland Police Department and let them know what was about to go down. Meanwhile, her son went out the back window and made tracks to the station house.

After the cavalry arrived, in the form of half a dozen police officers from this small municipality in Mobile County, Archie proceeded to terrorize Dianne for the next several hours, occasionally demanding that beer be brought to him from his truck by one of the officers. When he was ready to end it all for himself and his former wife, he demanded that one of the police officers present outside the house bring him his loaded shotgun from his truck. He stated that he wanted to kill his former wife with the shotgun before he killed himself. By the time this demand went out, Archie's buddy had sobered up enough to know that he didn't need to be anywhere near that house. And so he got the hell out of Dodge and surrendered to the posse.

Fortunately, the officer took a chance and, as he was approaching the window to the house where the crime was occurring, fired the shotgun at the defendant, aiming at his shoulder on the opposite side of where the defendant was holding a pistol to the victim's head. By the grace of God and good training, the blast hit the defendant right where the officer was aiming. The victim was not hit and she broke away while the other officers stormed the house and subdued the defendant.

The six officers personally witnessed all of the above actions. Additionally, the police dispatcher overheard the threats made by Archie, because early in the siege he had demanded that Dianne call the police and directed them to notify a local television station so that he could tell the world how he had been mistreated. And then he planned to execute Dianne on live television. The dispatcher did not notify the station, but did keep the line open so that she could monitor what was being said in the room where Archie was holding Dianne and her baby. Dianne had the good sense to not hang up the telephone. Also, to make matters worse for himself, Archie took the stand at trial and was totally obnoxious, perjured himself on major points and was thoroughly impeached by me with a court transcript from an earlier proceeding.

Archie handled that little problem simply by accusing me, the police and the court reporter at that proceeding of manufacturing from whole cloth his prior sworn statements. I couldn't have asked for a trial with more, or better evidence, nor one that tried as well as this one. This wasn't tantamount to shooting fish in a barrel; it was more akin to shooting a whale in a Dixie cup. The trial of Archie Nelson was the *only* case I have ever tried where I said, flat out, that the jury absolutely would find the defendant guilty.

But as the Good Book says: "Pride goes before a fall." The jury returned a verdict of Not Guilty in about fifteen minutes. When the foreman read the verdict form, I don't know whose jaw dropped quickest – mine, the defendant, his attorney, the spectators or the judge. I left three men on that jury who had been divorced, foolishly thinking that even they would find Archie Nelson's actions to be beyond the pale. I learned to never again underestimate the vitriol of a divorced man toward his former wife. But that still left nine male jurors who had never been divorced. They proved themselves to be either closet misogynists or absolute moral cowards.

The defense attorney was an adequate trial attorney, but he had been around many a courtroom in South Alabama and obviously was not at all naive about human behavior and what makes people tick. He used every strike he had on women. I'm certain, however, that he was merely trying to give his client a fighting chance, regardless of how ephemeral that chance might be. He had common sense, and I guarantee you, if pressed for an opinion before trial as to the chances of his client being acquitted, would have said two: slim and none, and slim just left town.

I just had to know whatever it was that passed for reasoning in the minds of those twelve candidates for retroactive birth control. Since this was the last trial of the week, I followed local custom and hot-footed it to the jury assembly room with the six officers and the Chief of the Saraland Police Department in tow. Another lesson learned shortly after my entering the jury room: After a tough loss, wait three days to regain your composure, and then wait one more just to make absolutely certain that you don't do or say something you might later regret. Not a single one of my jurors would look me in the eye. I simply surveyed the room and said one word: "Why?" One of these knuckle-dragging moral and intellectual pygmies responded: "Well, I guess this was just one of them things."

And, of course, I couldn't just let pass that brilliant *raison d'etre* for finding a palpably guilty defendant not guilty, without stirring the pot just a bit. I figuratively saw the words leaving my mouth, knew that I was really stepping in it, but still was unable to stifle myself. "Well, I just hope that nobody ever puts a gun to your wife or daughter's head." The reaction was explosive and virtually instantaneous. *Not* from Casper Milquetoast, but from some bearded, burly truck driver who looked as if he had been black-balled by the Hell's Angels because of his antisocial attitude and habits.

This gorilla, who I had foolishly perceived as a kick-ass, take-no-prisoners kind of a beer and shot guy, but one who would not appreciate for an instant a weasel the likes of Archie Nelson beating up on any woman, mounted a charge against me from across the amazing, shrinking jury assembly room. He was screaming at me with the volume and voracity of a wounded grizzly bear. "You ain't got no right! You ain't got no right!" Ignoring the offensiveness of his grammatical construction, not to mention the cacophony of roars being emitted by him, he was big enough and tough enough to break me in half. And no doubt would have, had it not been for the speedy intervention of about six or seven members of the Saraland Police Department. Those fine officers circled me like yaks fighting off wolves, and King Kong veered off at the last second.

By this time, I had both hands in my pants pockets, and was reassuring the charging beast that he was correct, "I *don't* have no right." Mighty Joe Young continued his monosyllabic verbal assault by letting everyone within hearing distance – the entire second floor of the courthouse in this instance, that: "It was the cops' fault; they should've killed that sum'bitch when they had the chance." (I ask you; could I even begin to fabricate this material?) Wishing to continue living, notwithstanding the bravery of the boys in blue from Saraland, I immediately apologized to this living testament to the existence of the long-postulated "missing link."

Unfortunately, my transparently insincere apology only succeeded in reducing the blood lust of the creature. After cursing me for a few more seemingly interminable seconds, he chose to reveal his true self to everyone involved by being a total weenie and ratting me out to the judge, who had long since sought refuge in his chambers. Sure enough, about fifteen minutes after King Kong/Oscar Meyer whined to Judge Teddy McDermott, I received a message from the good judge's bailiff to please come visit the judge in his chambers. I felt sure that at a minimum, a good ass chewing was going to claim me as its target, and that possibly, I might be held in contempt and placed in the cooler for the remainder of the afternoon.

After knocking on Judge McDermott's closed door and being told to enter, I took a deep breath and made my entry, fully prepared to suffer the wrath of McDermott. I spoke first, starting with as sincere an apology as I could muster, and segued into an acknowledgment that I was guilty of all charges and specifications, and that if the judge would only allow me an opportunity to get my toothbrush, I was ready for the lockup. Judge McDermott, bless his heart, just smiled and asked me to sit down. At least if I fainted, I wouldn't fall too hard and far to the floor. He then told me that everyone in the courtroom – himself, the defense attorney, the defendant and certainly every member of the jury knew that Archie Nelson was guilty as hell, but for whatever reason, they just didn't want to convict him.

He then told me that sometimes these things just happened, and that it was a total waste of time and effort to attempt to make sense of such an irrational act. And that was it! Though that case still sticks in my craw, I learned that when dealing with human beings, rational thought sometimes just doesn't enter the picture in the decision-making process. It's a lesson that I've never forgotten in trying a case. Most of the time, a jury follows the law, evaluates the facts and comes out with the proper verdict. Notice that I didn't say the "right" verdict, because sometimes people go to trial and the prosecution doesn't have sufficient credible evidence to prove a defendant guilty beyond a reasonable doubt. Sometimes guilty men are acquitted, and sometimes innocent men are convicted, although these occasions are far fewer than your average criminal defense attorney – particularly a crusading "true believer" – would have you believe.

Other than my stunning loss to the likes of Archie Nelson, there were plenty of victories – guilty verdicts – that I earned and attained during my relatively brief tenure in the Mobile County District Attorney's Office. One that was particularly meaningful to me personally and to society in general was that of Michael Otis Mitchell, perhaps the most dangerous child molester I ever prosecuted. Mitchell had already been indicted by the time I had received the case to prosecute.

The original prosecutor, Chris Hargett, had accepted a job with another office, and had given me the case file with the admonition to do whatever it took to convict Mitchell, because he was a bomb waiting to explode. Mr. Mitchell, it seems, liked young boys, and not in the fashion of any way acceptable, legal or moral in a civilized society. His M.O. – *modus operandi* or method of operation for you non-T.V. watching few – was to distribute very sloppily written and obviously unprofessional, generic "letters" to the parents of young boys, with his name and telephone number listed on the letter.

He represented himself to be a child psychologist who specialized in the counseling of young boys with regard to their sexuality and "reports" that the young boy had been observed in public exposing himself. He would individualize these letters and mail them, or otherwise deliver them, to the mothers of young boys who lived near him. And he also offered his services to "counsel" the young lads about their problems. Amazingly, none of these individuals, to my knowledge, called the police. Ultimately, the inevitable occurred; Mitchell grabbed a little boy, Kurt, who was all of six or seven years old, from the boy's yard and then took him behind a house on the same street and sodomized him, both anally and orally. Fortunately, the young boy ran home immediately and told his mother. She notified the police, who promptly arrested this scum who tried to pass himself off as human, instead of the Ebola virus that he actually was.

Mitchell's attorney managed to have the trial continued for more than a year, hoping that Kurt or his mother would grow tired of waiting and lose their commitment to prosecute him. I used this time to gather as much possible evidence as I could against him. I had received word from somebody familiar with Mitchell that he had had a girlfriend about the time he was arrested. I put our investigative staff on the job and they located her in Louisiana and persuaded her to return to Mobile for an interview. She proved to be a goldmine of information.

As it developed, she told us what a complete weirdo Mitchell was, – and wasn't that a shock – and how she tumbled onto the notion that perhaps their relationship wasn't exactly normal and certainly not good for her. I never said that she was a candidate for *MENSA*. But she was candid, not any kind of molester herself and a font of observations which provided us with sufficient information to obtain a search warrant for Mitchell's mother's house where he had lived prior to his arrest. Hidden in the attic was an assortment of young boys' clothes, some with blood stains on them. We were never able to connect these clothes to any child, alive or otherwise, but their unexplained presence bothers me to this day.

Perhaps even more disturbing, particularly in light of the clothes, was an assortment of index cards, spelling out various tortures and hideous "surgical" procedures intended for young boys. One of those index cards referred to Kurt by name as well as a directive to himself to commit a particular sexual act on Kurt, that act being precisely what he was charged with doing to Kurt. We obtained a court order for obtaining handwriting exemplars from Mitchell, and at trial presented expert testimony from a handwriting analyst that the writing on the index card and the writing in the exemplars were made by the same individual. The jury found Mitchell guilty. His plans, dreams, and fantasies of continuing to molest, and perhaps torture and kill little boys, were dashed – forever I pray.

At sentencing, crusty old Judge Telfair Mashburn, he of the flowing white mane, which caused him to resemble a patriarch of the Old Testament who exercised his iron will in guiding his flock of nervous and frightened sons and daughters of Israel, gave every appearance of being God's personal representative. Prior to his pronouncing Mitchell's punishment, he asked the defendant the traditional question of whether he had anything to say before learning of his fate. Mitchell indicated that he had nothing to say. Judge Mashburn, however, had a pronouncement of his own to make: "Mr. Mitchell, it is crimes like yours that make me deeply regret that the Supreme Court abolished the death penalty for rape and like crimes. Because you, sir, so richly deserve to die in the electric chair. But the law says that the most serious penalty that I can impose is a life sentence. And I hereby sentence you to serve life in the penitentiary."

I am happy to report that when the courtroom deputy was escorting the prisoner to the lockup, Mitchell began screaming, crying and tearing out his hair. His display of *machismo* did not go unappreciated by spectators and courtroom personnel. For several years after his incarceration, Mitchell wrote to me, attempting to persuade me that it was all a big mistake, and that he never hurt Kurt, that he actually loved him. To this day, I check at least twice each year on his status, and if am still alive, I will appear before the parole board and see to it that he never breathes free air again, even if he lives to be one hundred.

One more case with which I was totally uninvolved, but which begs to be told, was prosecuted by Teresa Tanner after I pulled up stakes and headed for the Jefferson County DA's Office in Birmingham. I refer to it as the "Community Killin'" case. At some point in 1985, I believe, perhaps a month or so before Christmas, a young woman named "Karo", had her butt thoroughly whipped by her man "Booker T." This particular offense was not the first butt whuppin' that "Booker T" had inflicted on Karo, only the most egregious. Similar occurrences had taken place over the course of the preceding months, and Teresa had told Karo – who always insisted on dropping the charges once they reached court – that there would be no more dropping of charges. The aggressive Miss Tanner had become become Karo's champion in attempting to prosecute these offenses in her role as victim counselor, part of every prosecutor's job, but which was taken very seriously by some, and totally ignored by others.

Unfortunately for Karo and most of her family, Booker T did not change his abusive ways, and events took their own course, which resulted in his being a poster boy for any interest group which is opposed to the Second Amendment. For you constitutionally challenged individuals who flunked high school civics, that is the right to bear arms. Another episode of violence occurred in late 1985 and Karo, predictably, made it known when she came to court that she wished not to pursue the matter. Teresa refused to drop the charges and the judge took it upon himself to dismiss the case, based on the victim's stated intention not to cooperate. That precipitous action by the judge had mixed results. Several weeks after the court dismissed the charges, Mobile's population was reduced by one due to the dismissal. Also, the size of the court docket increased by about a dozen, directly as a result of the population reduction.

You guessed it; Booker T represented the reduction in the population of Mobile, while Karo and assorted grandparents, grandchildren, aunts and uncles caused the increase in the size of the docket. As they say in my little corner of heaven, otherwise known as "The Heart of Dixie:" "Ya'll just ain't gonn'a believe this, but if I'm lyin', I'm dyin.'" Not too long after Judge Byrd dismissed the charges against Booker T because Karo requested that they be dropped, Booker T got drunk again and thoroughly whipped Karo's rear end. He also burned her with cigarettes, and amused himself in other ways designed to inflict as much pain as possible on his very own woman. She proved to be not quite the hapless and helpless creature that she had appeared to be up to that seminal moment in her life.

Something inside Karo snapped and she proceeded to do what she would not allow the judicial system to do. She upped the ante considerably. In fact, she took a small army of relatives with her on the night that she forever eliminated the possibility that Booker T would ever again abuse her like a mangy yard dog. The end result, while probably the kind of vermin extermination that might otherwise have concluded with her being awarded the key to the city and an honorarium from the community, resulted in her and more than a dozen others in the clan of avengers being prosecuted for murder.

As I indicated earlier in this vignette so emblematic of Mobile, Karo recruited at least half her family, old and young, men and women, boys and girls to accompany her as they made their way in stealthy fashion across back yards and scaling fences in order to surprise Booker T. As it turned out, they could have organized a Mardi Gras parade and Booker T would have been none the wiser, because he was passed out on the floor of his abode, a victim of that demon rum. At least his condition of being in a drunken stupor saved him from the certainty of the pain that followed.

Because when Karo and her vigilantes arrived, one or more pistols in their joint possession, they so thoroughly ventilated the prone body of Karo's tormentor that he looked like a piece of chocolate Swiss cheese by the time that the shoutin' and shootin' stopped. I believe that the magic number of shots fired into his worthless body was thirty-seven, but I could be off by one or two brass jacketed lead projectiles. But whatever the exact count, Booker T had become a receptacle for used metal when the smoke cleared. The situation became problematic only when it came to light that the older folks had passed the weapons to the kids after taking their shots, and let the little urchins blast away at the villain. No doubt so that they could feel as if they too were part of the family. When the homicide cops and the deputy coroner arrived, it seemed like an exercise in stating the obvious when they pronounced the body "DRT," also known in North Georgia as well as in parts of Alabama as, "Dead Right There."

Not too many citizens mourned the sudden, yet inevitable, passing of the low life, about which homicide detective John Wayne Boone (no kidding) was quoted in newspapers across the state the next day: "Booker T needed killing." And had it not been for the adults introducing the children to the time-honored tradition of the philosophy that some people just need to be dealt with outside the niceties of the judicial system, the whole bloody mess probably could have been handled in municipal court with the appropriate charge, discharging firearms within the city limits.

But there was that messy detail about passing the pistol to the juveniles and letting them take part in the turkey shoot. Some mistakes just can't be undone. None of the big dogs in the DA's Office wanted any part of what they deemed to be a sure loser in the courtroom. Since Teresa had been Karo's champion when Booker T was whuppin' up on her on a regular basis, let her be the one to prosecute Karo and all of her relatives, went the reasoning of the courtroom big shots who didn't want to sully their hands with the likes of what they perceived as a sure loser. And thus it was that Teresa took the case that made her reputation and solidly established her credentials as one of the meanest "trial dogs" on the porch.

And she tried that case about a dozen times, since the Alabama judicial system didn't allow joinder of defendants at that time. Some of the defendants were tried as juveniles, some certified and tried as adults and the rest as adults because they were at least eighteen at the time of the offense. Every last revenge-seeking soul among them was convicted, and they all received prison time, depending on their age and degree of involvement. Any chance of successfully invoking the "he needed killin'" defense was effectively nullified by the fact of the adults bringing in the young'uns to help with the termination of BookerT. And a star –Miss Teresa – was born. After establishing herself as queen of the courtroom in Mobile, she married Max Pulliam a year or so later and within another year or two joined me in the Jefferson County DA's Office where I had started working in January of 1985.

COURTROOM CHARACTERS AND THE STUFF THAT MADE THEM LEGENDS

I WOULD BE DERELICT if I failed to mention some of Mobile's finest criminal defense barristers, as well as a few other courthouse commandos. Robert Clark, better known as "Cowboy Bob" was one of those unforgettable characters who actually lived up to his image. From the top of his Stetson hat to the soles of his lizard-skin boots there was nothing phony about the man. He had a salt and pepper beard which actually looked good on him and served to enhance his

Central Casting looks. He was aggressive, tough as chewed leather, and if sufficiently provoked, would spit in Satan's face and challenge him to settle it in the back alley like a man. Or, if Old Scratch weren't available, he'd take on any mere mortal who didn't have the good sense not to provoke him. He also was a straight shooter and a worthy adversary.

His proudest days had been with United States Marine Corps in the early '60s, and like Marines throughout the world, he considered himself to be a marine until he walked among the angels, as the Army and the Navy looked on Heaven's scenes, while he and his fellow marines guarded the streets of that celestial place. Courtroom legend has it that no judge – state, federal or municipal – will schedule any trial or hearing involving the old marine on the tenth day of November of every year, because that date is the birthday of the Corps. Cowboy Bob would sooner be jailed for contempt than to ignore such a holy day of obligation. That story may be apocryphal, but it's been told so many times around the courthouse and among barristers at their favorite after-work watering holes, that it's yet another example of the legend becoming the truth.

The man in the lizard skin boots was just about as well known for his notorious, and somewhat spurious, "Rules of Court" as he was for his love of the Corps. Those rules display the cynicism for our system of justice that only a long-time insider can appreciate completely. As follows, the "rules" read:

(1) All defendants are guilty.

(2) All cops lie.

(3) Every prosecutor, defense attorney and judge is aware of the truisms contained in rules (1) and (2).

(4) *Some* cops *don't* lie.

(5) Except in dope cases, and then review rules (1) and (2).

For the record, even though I find the rules amusing and reflective of a defense attorney's mentality to a significant extent, my personal experience with police officers and agents has been that, contrary to Rule (2), most sworn officers tell the truth, even to the point where a lie would serve them much better than the truth. But, without question, Rule (1) is right on the money at least ninety per cent of the time. And that's all there is, folks, at least regarding your average man or woman on the street having a working knowledge of how the criminal justice system actually works, and *not* what is written in a primer on the legal system.

If you think that I was merely indulging myself in trial lawyer hyperbole about Cowboy Bob and his pugilistic prowess, let me relate to you a for real, no kidding, no BS courthouse account of what the Cowboy did to the spouse of a witness in the process of being hammered on cross examination by the man in the Stetson hat and the lizard-skin boots. This particular event occurred after I had left the balmy shores of Mobile Bay – not to mention the zany residents of the County Courthouse – but I believe that reports of said incident made about every newspaper in the state.

If memory serves me correctly, Clark was representing a woman against her former husband in a civil fraud action concerning some real estate. It culminated with a jury trial, Judge Braxton Kittrell presiding. Kittrell had been represented by Clark in at least two of his divorces, but everybody knew about the relationship and also knew that he cut Clark no slack in the courtroom. The new wife was on the witness stand giving her testimony, and Cowboy Bob was giving her unshirted hell. At some point during the inquisition of the witness, her new husband – formerly married to Clark's client in the pending action – took umbrage at the distinctively ungentlemanly abuse being heaped upon her by the old gunslinger himself.

When the heat had reached the boiling point, the knight in shining armor rose from his courtroom pew, and told the judge that he objected to the manner in which that "jerk," referring to Clark, was treating his wife. The old leatherneck, though taken aback, invited Sir Galahad to step outside and settle it like men, a challenge that was answered in the affirmative by the guardian of the woman being cross-examined. Dumb move; talk about waving a red flag in front of a fighting bull. Imagine one of our little Nipponese brothers waving the Rising Sun in the face of John Wayne in *The Sands of Iwo Jima*. Civility might not have been dead in Judge Kittrell's courtroom at that moment, but it was about to endure a severe beating.

In full view of the presiding judge and a rather surprised jury, the soon-to-be-hurting husband, and Cowboy Bob Clark, the very reincarnation of Chesty Puller, with the Eagle, Globe and Anchor and the honor of the Corps driving him to never retreat, went marching toward their own showdown outside the courthouse. And it was at this juncture, near the counsel table, that the aggrieved husband made his second big mistake. He sucker-punched a man who had been taught by experts in the art of both throwing and receiving such an attack, those being the men who kicked ass and took names at the lovely summer camp at Parris Island, South Carolina, lessons never forgotten by a Marine. The result of his rather imprudent actions was that he very quickly found himself in the position of being flat on his back while Cowboy Bob furiously pounded his face.

And that's when things really got interesting. The new wife, shrieking as she launched herself from the witness stand, took off on the dead run to save her man. In full stride she grabbed an umbrella from counsel table, leaving a speechless Lloyd Copeland (Cowboy Bob's trial partner) in her wake. And a wake nearly had to be held for her "protector" because, in addition to the pounding he was taking at the hands of Clark, she almost decapitated the poor man with Copeland's umbrella. It popped open as she was swinging it at the Cowboy with the result being that she missed Clark, but made solid contact with one of her sweety's eyes. About that time, the cooler heads of the court bailiffs prevailed and the two participants in Mobile's version of the old Gillette Friday Night fights terminated their antics with a few well-directed insults.

And now the kicker: Once order had been restored, Judge Kittrell polled the members of the jury in order to determine whether they could put aside the image of the fracas and still return a fair verdict. Not a single juror indicated that he could not put aside the brawl, neither party requested a mistrial, and the testimony just picked up where the aggrieved husband challenged the Cowboy to a few rounds in the ring. He was left with one good eye and a badly bruised ego. Oh, yes, his new wife lost the jury decision to the tune of about 175K. Just another day in Paradise at the Mobile County Courthouse.

As colorful as Cowboy Bob was, and still is, he couldn't top an old courthouse rat named Don "Big Daddy" Brutkiewicz. "Big Daddy" was a walking caricature of *Homo sapiens*. He was more than six feet tall, had at least eighty-eight teeth in his ever smiling mouth and his arms were so long that his knuckles dragged the floor. He also knew where most of the bodies were buried in the annals of Mobile politics and "business." Truth be told, he probably helped to bury at least half of them himself. In addition to his physical characteristics, he had certain courtroom practices that caught the attention of every lawyer who ever tried a case against him.

These peculiarities included his never carrying a brief case or anything even remotely resembling a file into the courtroom when trying a case. "Big Daddy" was notorious for walking into court for trial armed with nothing but his wits, experience and more-than-formidable knowledge of human nature. These attributes were powerful weapons indeed, particularly against inexperienced prosecutors who often were hit by the arrows in "Big Daddy's" quiver before they even realized that he had pulled the bow string. Upon ambling into the arena, he would promptly borrow one sheet of yellow legal-sized paper and a pen from the prosecutor, and would doodle on the paper and then wad it up during the course of a trial. Such an exercise, while rather strongly discouraged in most trial advocacy courses, only served to focus "Big Daddy's" attention.

He never missed a trick when a jury was present, and he knew how to pick 'em. He was at his absolute best when representing some street thug or second story man who just happened to be caught leaving the scene of a break-in with an armful of swag. "And you were just minding your own business when Junebug came running down the street and handed you that television set?" And if you weren't careful, he'd crack jokes for the jury's benefit, and almost crawl into the box with them if he thought that he could get away with it.

People that he talked with were "Pal" to him, an endearing salutation one might mistake for familiarity – except that he talked with everybody in the courthouse, and on the streets, pool halls and bars of the Port City. Some of his best clients, after all, came to him as a result of these conversations and from those locales. "Big Daddy" was not impressed in the slightest by the so-called "important" people. He would treat the Duke of Windsor in the same way that he would treat the courthouse janitor. They both were just "Pal" to him, except that the janitor would receive a bit more from him in the way of courtesy, against the day that he might need a favor from the janitor.

One incident in particular of "Big Daddy's" irreverence toward authority managed to make me a willing participant and still remains one of my lasting memories of Mobile. It seems that on this day I was handling the docket in the now late Judge Michael Zoghby's courtroom. All of the cases set for trial that day ended up with guilty pleas or continuances for one reason or another. All except one, that is. Brutkiewicz had one set for trial but he wanted to put it off for another day in the fashion of all good criminal defense attorneys who realize that delay is almost always an aid to their client's possible freedom.

Judge Zoghby was talking with several distinguished-looking black gentlemen, all dressed in suits, at the front of the courtroom and the good judge sent me into the hallways looking for "Big Daddy" in order to find out what Mr. Brutkiewicz intended to do with the pending case. Well, after finding the wandering barrister, he told me that he just wasn't sure what he wanted to do, obviously preserving all of his options. I related this cryptic message to Judge Zoghby who was still talking with the gentlemen of color.

Playing this game for several round trips between Brutkiewicz and Zoghby, I felt like a tennis ball after an extended volley; and I was also more than slightly irritated with Judge Zoghby for not making a decision, letting Brutkiewicz call the shots. After about the third trip, with no end in sight, I repeated for the benefit of the court what "Daddy D" had said to me on my last trip in search of a resolution. The judge asked me what Mr. Brutkiewicz had said, and I repeated it verbatim to the judge and his guests. "Mr. Brutkiewicz said that "he'd do whatever the rich white folks wanted him to do." Had Judge Zoghby been black, he would have turned white. As it was, he just turned from a man with a slightly swarthy complexion, to one with the color of the purest milky white alabaster. The men who really were black understood the satirical nature of the response, and seemed to get a good chuckle from it and from Judge Zoghby's obvious shock and discomfiture. But the judge's reaction was another story.

After hastily excusing himself from the company of his visitors, he directed me to find Brutkiewicz – chop, chop – and to report with "Big Daddy" to His Honor's chambers. After I fetched the other offender both of us went into the inner sanctum and prepared for our expected ass chewing. However, both of us knew that the gentle judge could neither bark that loudly nor bite that viciously. When we presented ourselves to the judge, the first thing that he said, and the only part of his remonstrance that I remember was: "Mr. McGregor and Mr. Brutkiewicz, do you have any idea that those men control the votes of three thousand citizens of this county?" "Daddy D" and I were biting our lower lips so hard to avoid bursting with laughter, it's a wonder that we didn't need a blood transfusion.

As I earlier indicated, the rest of the good judge's upbraiding of us is merely a blur. When we were dismissed from his chambers after a few more minutes, it was all that we could do to hold back the floodgates until we hit the hallway. And there, we doubled over with laughter pouring out of us so forcefully it hurt. Word of our social and political *faux pas* quickly made the

rounds in the courthouse, but that's as far as it went. And Judge Zoghby was comfortably reelected the next time the voters went to the polls, with no discernable reduction in the number of votes cast for him in the wards "controlled" by Judge Zoghby's visitors.

BATTLIN' BOB

YOU WOULD THINK, I imagine, that after my thorough exposure to the rather arcane culture and practices endemic to the Mobile

County Courthouse, and after observing the folly of fools other than myself, that I would be sufficiently inoculated against whatever it was that caused people to engage in risky or foolish behavior in and around the courthouse which invariably led to embarrassment. You would think. But then it wouldn't be Mobile and I wouldn't be me.

In mid-autumn of 1984, I had come to the realization that regardless of the ten years of courtroom experience that I had acquired in the previous twelve months, Mobile would never be my home and I wanted to return to Birmingham, Jefferson County. My plan hinged on David Barber's unseating the incumbent District Attorney in the upcoming election in that county, and then landing a position in his office. Piece of cake, and ultimately that is precisely what happened.

But prior to my plan's coming to fruition, the curse of Mobile stepped out and kicked me right in the groin. I learned many lessons from the painful experience, the primary one being to not do anything stupid on an otherwise slow news day. The boiling-over of the pot which led to front- page coverage in every major paper in the state had been simmering for months. And it stemmed from the well accepted practice– in some quarters – of certain members of the Mobile criminal defense bar's tendency to misuse the system and misrepresent facts to the court, or at least to stretch both the system and the facts to the breaking point, in order to keep one's client on the street "earning" money that he could pay to his attorney for this "service."

The other side of the equation is that I didn't go along with the program and had the bad manners to call a spade a spade and not a small shovel. It so happened that I was supposed to be trying a case on this particular occasion, one that had been continued by the court on several prior occasions at the request of the defendant's attorney.

My big mistake was embarrassing the defense attorney. Even worse, I handled the matter in open court on the record.

Before the lunch break that day, and not in the presence of the just sworn jury, I read into the court record the detailed notes that I had made at the last trial setting. That setting was continued because the defendant's attorney had made misrepresentations to the court, without benefit of my presence, about some imagined agreement with the State to pass the trial once again because I still had not complied with the standard discovery order.

Said attorney had made the mistake of not checking the court file prior to his complaining that the State had not complied with the Discovery Order. It contained a copy of a letter sent to him more than a year prior to the previous court setting by a prosecutor who had since left the office. She advised him in the letter that his discovery package was ready, and that he should pick it up at that prosecutor's office.

Unfortunately, the notes that I had made immediately following the last trial setting began with the following sentence: "Deen sleazed us again." And I was ticked off sufficiently to include it when I read into the record the rest of the notes that I had made on that occasion. Even though I gained some temporary satisfaction from reading that particular sentence into the official record, it was bad form on my part, to say the least. By doing that, I ceded the moral high ground to the opposition, which never pays off except in a real struggle to the death on a real battlefield.

My adversary in this battle of the Titans was Thomas Jefferson Deen III, a good lawyer who happened to practice with the redoubtable Cowboy Bob Clark. Jeff was a nice guy and a very good lawyer, but one whose quick wit, sharp tongue and facility for getting under the skin of prosecutors sometimes brought him dangerously close to the edge of the cliff as to what was acceptable courtroom decorum. He was also young, handsome and certain that he was God's gift to women as well as to the criminal justice system. As I said, he was young. He was also prematurely gray, but I was fat. He was wrong about being God's gift to the criminal justice system. I knew that I, not T. Jefferson Deen, was the chosen one. Although a few years older than Jeff, I too was young.

And based on what happened between us in the fall of 1984, maybe it was Deen who provided the template for Bob Clark's pugilistic prowess which took place at a later date. But no, in Clark's walloping of the aggrieved husband of the witness, he was responding in self defense. Deen sucker punched me. Without going into a detailed "who shot John," suffice it to say that the fracas occurred at the lunch break with no jurors present and with the judge in his office right next to the front of the courtroom where Jeff and I were standing while engaging in the ancient male ritual of: "My ----- is bigger than yours." I made the mistake of laughing at Deen while standing too close to him. I never saw Deen's version of the "bolo punch" coming until after his right fist made solid contact with my left ear. That is the moment when everything seemed to go into slow motion.

I could not believe what had just happened, even as my ear began to resemble a red cauliflower. Every instinct in my genetic makeup, going back to at least my Neanderthal ancestors, was crying out for me to wipe the floor with the body of one T. Jefferson Deen. My upbringing by a good momma and daddy, not to mention my instant realization that I could only make a bad situation worse by responding in kind, held my fists in check. I was no Rocky Marciano, nor even a fat and older version of Rocky Balboa, but I was a good three inches taller and forty pounds heavier than Mr. Deen. And I was mad enough to bite off his ear, years before Mike Tyson popularized that particular bit of savagery in his first bout with Evander Holyfield.

I thought, and still do, that I exercised remarkable restraint in merely grabbing Jeff by the throat with my left hand, and in the process pushing him about a foot back into the outer wall of Judge Zoghby's chambers. Since the wall was merely a cheap wooden facade, the judge had no problem hearing Jeff's body being slammed against it. I continued to hold him by the neck while he kept on attempting to throw punches with both hands, connecting with nothing but air, and looking for all the world like some cartoon character as he wind milled his air punches. Within seconds, Judge Zoghby and two police officers who were witnesses in the case, arrived at the ridiculous scene, and their presence caused a cessation of the hostilities.

Net result : one surprise punch thrown by Deen giving me a cauliflower ear for about a day, while he sported throttle marks around his throat caused by my grip around his pencil neck, along with a small scratch on his face caused by my thumb as I squeezed his wind pipe. But I never threw a punch. Actually, I exercised considerable restraint in not pounding Jeff's pretty face into something resembling a bowl of goo.

The gentle Judge Zoghby promptly declared a mistrial when Jeff refused to guarantee that the fracas wouldn't recur during the trial. And then Mr. Deen declared to one and all in the hallway immediately after leaving court that he had gotten what he wanted – a mistrial. If you didn't know Jeff, you might think, based on his hallway pronouncement that he got the mistrial that he wanted, that the entire episode was planned just to avoid trying the case for another few months. Knowing him as I did, it was obvious to me that he was merely engaging in some face-saving braggadocio and certainly didn't walk into court that day planning his own version of Pearl Harbor on my ear. But his pronouncement of getting the mistrial that he wanted certainly didn't help prevent the firestorm of publicity that resulted once the news media was made aware of the "Thrilla from Mobilla."

Approximately fifteen minutes after the judge declared a mistrial, as I was sitting in my office going through my files and feeling my ear swell by the minute, Kathy Jumper of the *Press Register* called me on the 'phone, and directed some rather pointed inquiries to me concerning the pugilistics between Deen and me. Somebody apparently had broken a world record running for the telephone in order to tip off the daily fish wrapper. I have my suspicions concerning the identity of the tipster, but I can't say for a fact that this particular individual was the party responsible for the telephone inquiry. But I do know that Jeff Deen seemed to revel in the resulting publicity which started the next day, but soon took on a life of its own like some mutation of a nasty little germ. I simply told Ms. Jumper that the whole episode was "regrettable," and that it never should have occurred.

Regardless of who actually tipped off the reporter, it was inevitable that it would soon become public knowledge. I had no idea how inclusive the public would be, however. And over the next several days I learned one of life's very valuable lessons: never screw up on a slow news day. Your screw-up will expand geometrically, and you'll live with it for years. The next day's edition of the *Press Register* carried a front page account of what it labeled a "free swinging brawl." I never threw a punch in this so-called "brawl." I simply pinned the pugnacious Mr. Deen to the wall with my hand clasped firmly around his neck. The entire rooster fight lasted no more than a few seconds. In addition to the *Press Register*'s account of the shoving match, several of the other major papers in the state, including the Birmingham *Post Herald* apparently had nothing better to write about that day except the punch heard round the world in Judge Zoghby's courtroom the previous morning.

You might think that the extensive coverage by the print media would be sufficient to satisfy the blood lust of the electronic media. You would be wrong. The holocaust was just beginning to smolder. That afternoon a local television pretty boy and a cameraman showed up outside my door. After initially telling the local imitation of Geraldo Rivera that I had nothing to say, other than a brief repetition of my one sentence statement of regret for the *Press Register*, the pale imitation of Geraldo informed me that if I refused to make a statement for the viewing audience, he would pull a Mike Wallace and have his cameraman focus on my closed door, while he, the news flack, commented on my refusal to comment on the courtroom "brawl." I weighed the plusses and minuses of the situation, and then gave a very innocuous statement to the effect that "it was a regrettable incident that shouldn't have happened." This was pretty much what I had told the reporter for the *Press Register*.

Too bad that my sparring partner, Mr. Deen, opted for the low road in his response. You would think that even a one-alligator town like Mobile, Alabama could find something more important to air on its six o'clock Saturday news than a rooster fight between a mouthpiece for the guilty and a middle-aged, fat deputy prosecutor. But then, you've probably never been to Mobile, where only the briefest of stays would convince you otherwise. But as sure as the old maxim that "no good deed goes unpunished," that Saturday evening news account of the battle of Judge Zoghby's courtroom was treated as the biggest event since the bombing of Pearl Harbor.

The video began with my meek statement of regret, but rapidly escalated into the Jeff Deen Comedy Hour, with Deen in his sweats crouching in front of the YMCA, shadow boxing to the tune of the theme from the movie *Rocky*, while proclaiming to the entire Bay Area that: "I'll zealously defend my clients any time that I go to court." This performance resulted in the public's taking renewed interest in the entire silly confrontation. Worse, it kept the disciplinary committee of the Mobile Bar Association attuned to the ongoing silliness.

It peaked the following Monday and Tuesday when, as a joke, Cowboy Bob Clark drafted a "Motion to Compel the Prosecutor to wear Thumbless Gloves." It would have been funny but for the fact that Clark neglected to tell in sufficiently forceful language, his fourteen year old runner who filed pleadings for him, that it was a joke meant for my eyes only. You guessed it; the runner actually filed it in the clerk's office. It may have provided some mirthful moments for our colleagues, as well as more grist for the *Press Register* news mill, but neither I nor the Bar Association saw much humor in it.

Judge Ferrell McRae, presiding Circuit Judge at the time, held Clark in contempt, fined him $50, and made Clark give a public apology in McRae's courtroom. Other than that, and the inevitable press coverage of the apology, the entire comedy of bad judgment, assault and the tsunami generated by all of this nonsense, the wood was in the shed and all appeared to have survived it without permanent scarring of our individual and institutional reputations.

Except for one small matter which emerged a couple of days after Clark's apology; the Disciplinary Committee of the Bar Association notified both Deen and me that each of us was the subject of a complaint to the Bar. Of course, I handled this matter in my usual calm and reflective manner, i.e. I went absolutely ballistic. I called, among other people, the president of the Mobile Bar Association as well as the attorney appointed to investigate this "stain" on our profession, and the head of the State Bar Disciplinary Committee. I wanted to know who had filed this obviously scurrilous and patently false complaint. Ultimately, I was told, and I believed it, that any incident involving members of the Bar which might bring discredit on the profession, must result in the Disciplinary Committee itself filing a complaint and conducting a formal investigation. (Some people might say that would be akin to calling a whore a woman of low morals, but that's just some people.)

And so for the next several weeks, I carried an extra load of guilt and worry with me, until the Mobile Bar Association and then the Alabama State Bar gave me a clean bill of health. I'll never forget what an old courthouse legend named H.R. "Bubba" Marsal, who was still a bull of a man, told me as I was being interviewed by the Disciplinary Committee, of which he was a member: "Hell, Tiger, we used to settle our courtroom disagreements right on Canal Street." Obviously, times had changed, but it was crystal clear where Bubba's sentiments lay. Notwithstanding the clearing of my name and reputation, however, I must still report the complaint every time that I turn around, whether for federal security clearance, various state regulations or purchasing a Good Humor bar on credit. And for at least the next decade, I was saddled with the sobriquet "Battlin' Bob" every time that I entered a courtroom, an appellation that wasn't all bad, depending on the circumstances.

While all of the hoo-rah was going on in the courtroom, something far more important was occurring in the delivery room at Providence Hospital. John McAvoy McGregor, my son and firstborn, drew his first breath on the seventh day of September, 1984. Just like his old man, he was ten days late for the party and Molly had to be induced. Even the drug used to induce labor failed to do the trick and, ten hours after the first try, Johnny was still reluctant to abandon the security of his mother's womb for the unknown challenges that he would face in the world of the bottle and the breast. Dr. Chip Haines performed a Caesarean in introducing young Johnny to the world. He quickly became the center of our universe, and we had decided that we had experienced enough of Mobile and environs. I was ready to head back north and so was Molly. Johnny was just along for the ride.

Later that fall, a young career prosecutor in Birmingham named David Barber ran against the incumbent Jefferson County District Attorney, John DeCarlo. When Earl Morgan, the previous District Attorney retired, Barber was expected to succeed him as the county's top prosecutor. But the governor threw a wrench into Barber's plans and appointed Decarlo, then an appellate court judge. Seeing David as a potential threat to his election two years down the road, Decarlo followed the path blazed by his mentor and the man who appointed him to fill out Earl Morgan's unexpired term, that man being the legend himself, George Corley Wallace. And the "guv'na" could be absolutely ruthless in eliminating potential political rivals.

And so, John Decarlo's first order of business was to summon Mr. Barber into his office and inform him that his services to the citizens of Jefferson County would no longer be required, necessary or even wanted. In other words, "don't let the door hit you in the rear end on your way out, Mr. Barber." And with that one ill-considered act, he virtually ensured that David Barber would oppose him. Had he used a little more finesse, he would have called a press conference and

Embraced Barber publicly as the best *Assistant* District Attorney in Alabama, thus effectively knocking the wind out of Mr. Barber's sails. Had he taken that course of action, David likely would never have run against him.

Undeterred, David simply threw his hat into the ring in the next general election. He campaigned as an outsider who was a victim of politics. David was also very popular with the vast majority of police officers, as well as the general public, having been on the news in his official capacity on more than a few occasions. Come election time, he defeated Decarlo, in a runaway victory. I had not tried to play it safe in my support of David. I wrote both a nice check made out to his election committee and also wrote him letters, one before the election and one congratulating him for his victory. And shortly thereafter, I wrote him another letter, asking him to keep me in mind for a job should he have an open position available. I had picked the right horse to ride and David offered me a job shortly after assuming the mantle of power.

But before leaving Mobile, the criminal defense bar presented me with a boxing speed bag that was autographed by all of the usual suspects. Also, one of my last nights in Mobile was spent hoisting mugs of the golden brew with these same characters, most prominent of whom was that star of stage, screen and whatever boxing ring was available, T. Jefferson Deen himself. And whoever said that I'm not a good sport? Jeff and I remain friends to this day.

Some people not of the particular culture native to Mobile had urged me to file charges against Deen. But that would have marked me for the rest of my career as a "wuss" who actually sought relief from the very profession that put bread on my plate and diapers on my infant son. In other words, it would have been bad form of the worst kind, and I would have lost all respect from my colleagues. By handling the affront myself, without relying on the damned court system, my stature was enhanced in the eyes of my brothers and sisters in the Bar. And such was my sojourn in Mobile.

Chapter Four

BACK TO BIRMINGHAM – THE KINGFISH AND ME

JANUARY 3, 1985 IN Birmingham was as cold as a prosecutor's heart. It was also windy and just plain raw, particularly when having to walk about three blocks to the County Courthouse. And that is precisely what I was doing that day at about 8:00 in the morning ready to begin my new job as a deputy district attorney in Jefferson County. I was deemed suitable to fill one of the available slots, and David hired me as one of his supervisors. My time and record in Mobile had ensured that I would receive strong consideration for a supervisory position, and I was fortunate enough to land one.

Walking with me were two men, also new to the job, who would very quickly become close friends of mine, George Andrews and Paul Greene. George had been in private practice prior to coming to work for Barber and had previously been a prosecutor in the Bessemer District Attorney's Office for several years before his first tenure as a private practitioner. Paul had come directly from the Morgan County District Attorney's Office. Both of them were hired as supervisors by the boss, or "division chiefs" as our office nomenclature described our positions. And all three of us "newbies" were appointed to be division chiefs in the new administration. Of course, there were a few holdovers from the prior administration. But most of the experienced hands that went into practice for themselves during the DeCarlo administration elected to remain in the private sector.

A division chief in the Barber administration was in charge of a designated judge's courtroom, with either two or three deputy district attorneys working that courtroom under his/her supervision. The chief had the responsibility of reading over the case files of those cases that had been distributed by the Clerk of the Court to the various judges, and then assigning them to the attorneys in his charge. He also was in charge of ensuring that everything ran smoothly in court and that all dockets were covered by at least one of the assistants assigned to his court.

My draw was the recently appointed J. Richmond Pearson, a former state legislator and Assistant United States Attorney who was appointed by the governor to fill the open slot formerly occupied by Charles Crowder, who retired from the bench several months before I came aboard. Interestingly, the governor who appointed Pearson was George Corley Wallace, who for years in his various tenures as the state's chief executive, looked upon Pearson the legislator as a big burr under his saddle, a man he dearly wanted to see leave Montgomery.

Another burr under Wallace's saddle was the voting public of Jefferson County which included the city of Birmingham. Jefferson County never returned a majority vote for Wallace in his several bids for the governor's chair, a fact that he never forgot nor forgave. Crowder's retirement presented Wallace with a unique opportunity – a chance to rid himself and the legislature of the direct influence of Pearson, as well as an opportunity to once again stick it to Birmingham. And he jumped on it. Shortly thereafter, J. Richmond Pearson became the *Kingfish* of the Jefferson County Courthouse, and it was never the same, even unto this day, several years after his retirement.

Pearson's courtroom, or *coat room*, as he pronounced it, became a chamber of justice, horrors, unabashed laughter and frustration for lawyers during his stay on the bench. One thing it never became was dull. His Honor was a very large black man who had put on a great deal of weight since his playing days as a very slim, very talented baseball player. By the time that he ascended to the bench his playing days were long gone.

The very first thing that you saw upon entering his courtroom, on the wall where you couldn't miss it, was an oil painting of the Kingfish himself. His bench was to the right of that entrance, perhaps ten or so yards from the far end of the room where Judge Pearson presided from his bench. He just wanted to make sure that the location of his portrait was the first thing to hit your eye upon entry. Aesthetically, it was totally misplaced. Psychologically, it hit the bull's eye.

While it may be tempting to depict Judge Pearson as a caricature of every racist's warped vision of what all black judges look like and talk like, the reality of the Kingfish was far different. Depending on his audience, he could mangle the King's English or speak it like the finest orator ever to wear a barrister's wig at the Queen's Bench. He could "get down" with a brother from the "hood," or speak with courtesy and understanding to any cracker with a red neck who sought justice in his court. And, as long as a litigant gave the Court the dignity and respect that the law and decorum demanded, Judge Pearson treated that individual in reciprocal fashion.

Lawyers, of course, were held to a higher standard than were witnesses, defendants and casual observers. Point of fact is that JRP treated many lawyers on occasion about as well as a yard dog would be treated. But, it was never personal and anyone was subject to a Kingfish tirade if that person breached the Judge's sense of propriety and decorum or any of his very own "rules of court."

Given the fact that I was in his court much of each day all but guaranteed that I was his designated whipping boy. My first day in court removed any doubt that might have been in my mind as to who was in charge of the court. And it wasn't me, I can assure you. The chain of command was made manifest to me as I was representing the State in the taking of a plea of guilty before the Court. The law in Alabama, not to mention the other forty-nine states, is that either the defendant or the prosecutor must make a sufficient factual showing on the record before the judge is permitted to pronounce the defendant guilty. If the prosecutor makes an adequate factual showing, the defendant must assent to it on the record. Naturally, I waited until Pearson took a breath, and at the appropriate time during the plea *colloquy*, began my recitation of a factual summary of the crime.

This mantra is the hocus pocus recited by the judge to ensure on the record that the guilty plea is knowing, voluntary, unequivocal and without any hidden agreements between the prosecutor and the defense attorney made in order to get the defendant to plead guilty. It also must contain sufficient detail of the crime to ensure that the State indeed had sufficient evidence to convict should the matter go to trial. I got about three syllables out of my mouth before his Honor cut me off at the knees in his inimitable fashion: "Mr. McGregory, *(sic)* I will take a guilty plea without any help from you." His knowing mispronunciation of my last name was just one of my many buttons that he took great delight in pushing.

Instead of demonstrating that I was blessed with at least a modicum of common sense by keeping my mouth shut and my vocal chords inoperative, I proved once again that, given the choice between shooting myself in the foot and practicing the virtue of remaining silent under fire, I will fire that gun every time, maiming myself and any bystanders who happen to be in the vicinity. I compounded my original *faux pas* by pointing out to the sitting jurist that unless someone made a factual showing on the record, the guilty plea would be subject to either direct appeal or collateral attack down the road

And why would a defendant who was willingly pleading guilty later want to attack his guilty plea? Because the only eye witness to the crime died. Or because prison wasn't as pleasant as the local pool hall and beer joint. Or because the other cons convinced him that his lawyer sold him out, or... I think you get the picture. Judge Pearson must have taken scores of guilty pleas with absolutely no showing of a factual basis for the guilt of the defendant, but never had one come back at him, to my knowledge. I guess that he really did know how to take a guilty plea without any help from me. But that little clash with the Kingfish marked the first of more than a few disagreements between the two of us. And my success rate never changed – Kingfish one hundred, McGregory zero.

Instead of simply accepting my fate and realizing that I was about to engage in a battle that I had no chance of winning, I made up my mind to stand tall, be a strong advocate for the State and let the chips fall. In short, to stick out my Scots-Irish chin and let Pearson knock me on my hindquarters at every opportunity. And, being the slow learner that I am, both my chin as well as my hindquarters ached during most of my tenure in the Kingfish's court. Each day seemed to inspire another *Looney Tunes* episode from JRP's evidentiary rulings or his procedural innovations. At times I would laugh. Other occasions would bring tears to my eyes. And there were those times when I didn't know whether to laugh or cry, and so I did a little of both. One thing, however, never changed. The Kingfish was the man in charge, and woe be to any lawyer who seemed to forget that elementary fact.

And, sometimes his rulings would come straight from left field, directly to the plate, without even hitting the cutoff man. And the runner would be out, regardless of whether he had to slide or come in standing up. And any objections to the call would only ensure that the next three close plays would not go your way. One example, almost comical but for the gravity of the offense, became known as the great tape recorder caper.

Mike Anderton and I were trying a defendant for murdering his infant son. The defense attorney was Bill Clark, a West Point graduate and a bird colonel in the reserves at that time. He since has been awarded his star. Clark had a well deserved reputation as one of the best defense attorneys in Alabama. He would come at you in trial in waves, resembling nothing so much as Patton's Third Army sweeping across Europe. His trial personality, however, was less than electric. But he was relentless and always well prepared. And he also knew the rules of evidence as well as if he had written them himself.

He was not above stretching those rules to the breaking point, particularly before a judge who might be somewhat intimidated by his mien. And Judge Pearson, despite his ability to freeze a jigger of water into an ice cube with a mere glance, was just such a judge. Not that Clark himself served as the intimidator. Rather, it was his formidable reputation with the courts of appeal that caused the Kingfish to be a tad more deferential in his rulings on Clark's objections than he would toward 90 per cent of the bar.

But what Clark got him to do in this case almost blew out my aneurism like a defective tire after I stopped laughing and realized that the man was serious. Attorneys had given closing arguments on Friday afternoon and the judge had charged the jury as to the law. Since it was past five o'clock when he completed his jury charge, His Honor decided that the next morning would be a good time for deliberations to begin. Come 9:00 sharp the next morning, jury present and accounted for and in the jury room, and the Kingfish inquired as to whether the lawyers had any questions or requests.

My co-counsel Mike Anderton and I had taken care of all of our business on the previous afternoon, and thus had nothing to do until the opposition stated that it was ready to proceed, and Judge Pearson could tell the twelve that they could select a foreman and begin deliberations. Mike and I told the judge that we were ready to proceed, and then the Kingfish turned to a pensive Bill Clark.

Clark, after looking silently at the floor for about ten seconds, informed the man in the black robe that he had one additional objection to the myriad number that he had voiced during the trial. Fascinated as to what he could possibly come up with at this stage of the proceedings, Anderton and I almost fell over with laughter when our adversary objected to the tape recorder being sent to the jury room because "the recorder was not in evidence and thus shouldn't be sent back with the other exhibits."

Because the tapes of the defendant's statement had been properly authenticated and admitted into evidence, the tape recorder itself should be sent back with the exhibits in order that the jury might play the tapes if they so desired. Not allowing the tape recorder to go back to the jury room would be analogous to not allowing a light bulb be sent back to the jury room to replace one that had burned out. My initial reaction to the motion was one of amazement that Bill Clark actually had a sense of humor.

But I was doing no laughing at all when Judge Pearson actually ruled that the tape recorder would not go back to the jury room unless it was offered and admitted into evidence. And so a tape recorder just purchased for the use of every attorney and secretary in the office sat for more than a year in the Clerk's office with the other exhibits until the Court of Appeals affirmed the conviction and the State Supreme Court declined to review it.

When I told my boss about the court's ruling, he just slowly shook his head and walked away muttering to himself. I, on the other hand, comported myself with dignity and control over my baser instincts to tell Judge Pearson that he must have gotten his law degree from Kmart. No, being a person with steely control over his emotions, I merely went to my office, threw all my law books against the wall and screamed profanities during my entire tirade. It wasn't the lost tape recorder that caused me to snap; it was the sheer insanity of the ruling. But judges can be like that, and there's not a damn thing that a prosecutor can do about it.

The Kingfish also provided moments of levity, sometimes even at his own expense, although rarely with the intent of self-deprecation. The following episode is demonstrative of the humorous side of the law because J. Richmond Pearson finally met his match in court. The story immediately became part of courtroom lore and legend and is still told around various niches of the courthouse where coffee is drunk and lawyers talk about how much better things were "back in the day." This is one of those incidents. I wasn't there when it happened, but I read the transcript of the proceedings the next day. And some twenty or so years later, it's still talked about whenever tales of the Kingfish are told by barristers, young and old.

The short of it is that Lemuel Haywood, a real bad guy, who happened to be black, had been transported from Raiford Prison in Florida where he was serving a life sentence for some heinous crime, just one of several felony convictions attached to his lengthy criminal history. A robbery case had been pending against him in Jefferson County He had elected to challenge this pending charge on the grounds that he had been denied a speedy trial, and he had fashioned some fairly impressive legal arguments to buttress his motion. He represented himself in court with the presence of a veteran attorney, Ken Gomany, appointed to ensure that his rights were protected. As matters developed, it became evident that the only person in the courtroom who might require legal assistance was the Kingfish.

The proceedings began in a routine fashion with Judge Pearson making a few remarks for the record. At that point, he asked the prisoner why he was not in court at the previous setting, knowing full well that the man was serving a lengthy term in a state prison in Florida. The prisoner responded that he had been in prison, and thus could not make a court appearance in Alabama because he had not been transported there by the authorities. At which point he began to state the grounds for his motion to dismiss the Alabama charges for its failure to give him a speedy trial. But Judge Pearson was not finished with him and began hectoring the man, as he was wont to do on occasion, particularly with an obvious bad guy.

The prisoner/petitioner initially let the Kingfish's interruptions and badgering of him roll off his back. But, for once at least, Judge Pearson's seemingly unerring sense of sizing up a litigant failed him. He had pushed one button too many with this hardened convict, and the result was that for once in his judicial tenure, the Kingfish was not the King of his Court.

At some point when Judge Pearson was toying with Haywood as a cat might play with a captured mouse, Haywood reverted to type and became the bad guy who had terrorized the general community as well as the other bad guys in Raiford Prison. I guess he decided that he'd had enough of an overweight judge, a "brother"who'd made it, and was now amusing himself at the expense of a "brother" who hadn't. Haywood responded with a stream of racial invectives and imprecations worthy of any Grand Wizard of the Ku Klux Klan. I wouldn't even attempt to repeat some of his verbal assault on Judge Pearson; simply that all of it was appalling, and some of it was hilarious. At one point in his tirade, however, Haywood demanded to know what the judge intended to do to him for his outburst, put him on death row? Because that didn't scare him one bit since he already had been to death row on two different occasions.

Initially, Judge Pearson attempted to quiet the man, but soon realized the futility of his efforts. He let him finish and then told Haywood that he would get the speedy trial that had been denied to him, and that it would be tried first on Monday's docket, this being a Thursday. Bob Posey was the ADA in charge of the case and he had no idea where all the witnesses currently were located, much less whether any of them would remember the details of what had occurred.

But by the following day, Judge Pearson's famous sense of how to handle a difficult litigant had returned to him. He called Posey on the 'phone and informed him that upon further reflection of the legal arguments raised by Mr. Haywood, he believed that Haywood had indeed been denied a speedy trial and his motion to dismiss was hereby granted. By Monday, Mr. Haywood was well on his way back to Raiford Prison to resume his work as a prison lawyer while serving the rest of his life in that hell hole of Raiford Prison. Call it a draw, with Kingfish starting slowly, but using his ring smarts in the late rounds to score enough points to avoid a humiliating KO inflicted by Haywood.

My time with the Kingfish lasted for about a year. David Barber then rotated the prosecutors. Not that I was constantly in Judge Pearson's court during that year. If I was assigned a major case from another judge's docket, obviously I handled that case in that particular judge's court. By and large, however, the Kingfish and I were married to each other. And after I got used to the fact that he certainly wasn't going to change, if I wanted something done, I'd better find a way that was compatible with him and his "procedures". And after a few months service, I actually got to like Judge Pearson and to this day have great respect for his wisdom and common sense. My guess is either that I grew up a bit or that I became Exhibit A that the Stockholm syndrome really exists. I doubt seriously that I grew up, and so I'd have to put my money on the Stockholm syndrome manifesting itself.

Chapter Five

Making My Bones
Larry Steven Kimbrough – a Soldier of Fortune

Notwithstanding the vast experience and trial by fire that I had gained in the Circuit Courts of Mobile County, and in spite of my exceedingly high opinion of my own abilities as a trial attorney, I was looked at askance by some of my colleagues and had a reputation as "that guy from Mobile who gets into fights in the courtroom." Trial attorneys by nature and training are a skeptical lot, and if not, they don't win many cases. Thus, I was not surprised that I wasn't welcomed as the second coming of the Perry Mason of prosecutors. I knew that the only place that I could prove myself was in the courtroom and in a case where it mattered.

And those that mattered usually were the big cases where the defendant was patently guilty and the mouthpiece for the accused was one of the high-dollar boys who had the reputation and skins on the wall to match his fee. If it appeared that prosecution of a given case was equivalent to tugging on Superman's cape or spitting into the wind, all the better. And if the case had the cherry on top, a white defendant with a plot that would catch the eye of the print and video media, well you really couldn't ask for more – unless you lost the damned thing. And then all you would want would be a cold hamburger and a one-way bus ticket to nowhere, which is exactly where your career would be going.

Larry Steven Kimbrough proved to be the great white whale that I pursued like Ahab, but Melville's driven captain was possessed with an obsession that destroyed him in his lust to defeat the leviathan. I got my harpoon into Kimbrough and rid the seas of Jefferson County of a man willing to kill his business partner for money. And he was represented by the Lone Wolf himself, Lawrence Sheffield Jr. Sheffield could charm a raccoon out of a tree with a grin that would make Davy Crockett proud, or he could "out mean" a pack of junkyard dogs intent on doing grievous harm to anybody in the vicinity. He had a well-deserved reputation for being able to manipulate a jury as if its members were putty in his palm.

And in the only case prior to Kimbrough in which I took him on, he had beaten me like the proverbial red-headed step child. But he proved to be a good friend; after that beating, he took me out for lunch and gently pointed out a few things that he might have done differently. I think that he admired me for my tenacity and recognized my unpolished skills in court. There would be no free lunches courtesy of Mr. Sheffield during the Kimbrough investigation and subsequent prosecution. And, just for good measure, Sheffield's son, Lawrence III – a formidable adversary in his own right – was helping the old man, as if he needed help, which he most assuredly did not.

But back to Kimbrough. He was business partners with a man named Charley Land, terrific with machinery, a lost babe in the woods in his naiveté and inability to judge people for what they were and not what he wished that they were. Kimbrough knew next to nothing about machinery, engineering and/or inventions, but was a glib talker and an immoral con man. He was also a man who lusted for money and women and didn't much care about working for either. He preferred to take the fruits of someone else's labors – either in the bedroom with the wife of another man or through the proceeds of a large insurance policy on his partner's life.

Land and Kimbrough started a business together with two or three other individuals whose purpose was to build and then market a paper counting machine that was more efficient than anything then being sold. The name of the company was *Motion Industries*, and Land was to be in charge of the technical aspects of inventing and then building the counter, while Kimbrough would be the front man and attract investors and vendors. Their small company included several other people, mainly engineers, who were sufficiently impressed with the possibilities that they came on board in hopes of making the project a success, both as to the technology and its potential for making money for the group.

Land was a fairly gifted inventor and Kimbrough was a fairly gifted grifter. He also was lazy and immoral and would prefer to kill his partner for the proceeds of the $1million "key man" life insurance policy that he would collect upon his partner's death, rather than roll the dice on the future success or failure of the business. These types of policies are fairly common in the business world where each of two men is vital to the success of the business. If one of the partners comes to an untimely demise, the investment of the other is protected by the proceeds of the policy.

The plan makes good business sense – unless Larry Steven Kimbrough is your partner. A word of advice to the budding entrepreneur: Before you and your business partner purchase policies of this type, your life being insured with him as the beneficiary, make sure that you know and trust your partner *real* well. Charley Land just thought that he knew Kimbrough. Turns out that he didn't and his ignorance or misplaced trust almost cost him his life.

It happened one night near Leeds, Alabama, a city located within a short driving distance of Birmingham. Charles Land and a man named John David Strong were in Land's car driving to what Land thought was Strong's residence. It was the first time that they had actually met each other, but they had talked on several occasions on the telephone, each conversation having been initiated by Strong. Since Land was an inventor, Strong had contacted him with some bogus story about being an inventor himself and wanting Land's assistance with his (non-existent) invention. Land bit, and made arrangements to meet Strong in front of a Southside ice cream shop one seemingly pleasant summer evening.

Upon meeting Land, Strong – who could have passed himself off as the twin brother of G. Gordon Liddy – told Charley his design specifications were at a house in Leeds, but that they must first go to a house in Homewood, just a short drive from where they met, and pick up a sack with some of Strong's personal items. Land, notwithstanding a nagging foreboding about taking a drive at night with a stranger that he had just met, proceeded to do precisely that. And, were he not later struggling with Strong for his very survival, he might well have been found wearing a dress, and without the benefit of a beating heart. That last statement wasn't any lame attempt at humor. It literally was part of the plan that Strong had devised should his goal of killing Land come to fruition.

When they stopped at the house in Homewood, Strong told Land that he was staying at the house in a back bedroom and that he must fetch a paper bag that held some personal belongings. Strong disappeared for a few minutes behind the house – which served no purpose other than to provide some cover in the back-yard bushes for the sack and its contents – and reappeared in a few minutes with the paper sack. Charles Land was a very nice man, but far too trusting. And with sack in hand, the pair headed for Leeds, ostensibly for the specifications for Strong's "invention," but actually to find a remote area for Strong to carry out the single item on his actual agenda, that being the murder of Charles Land.

Land was driving his car with Strong riding shotgun. When they got to Leeds, Strong became vaguer in his directions to Land. He also began to insert his hand into the paper sack, a move which did not escape Land's notice. Long after most people would have detected something rotten in Denmark, Charley Land's hair on the back of his neck began to stand up. It was just about then that Strong's right hand started to come out of the sack clutching a .38 revolver, and Land finally decided that Strong wasn't what he claimed to be. He also decided that being shot on a lonely road in Leeds, Alabama was not on his agenda. Land released the steering wheel and grabbed for the gun with both hands as the car went swerving off the road.

The fear-induced adrenalin upsurge gave Land strength that I'm sure he didn't know that he possessed. The car went off the road during the struggle and came to a stop on the shoulder. All the while, Land was trying to get the gun from Strong while pummeling him with one fist and then the other. During the melee Strong was laughing at Land's efforts. Finally, Land broke loose from the clutches of Chuckles the Hit Man and was able to escape by getting the front door open. As he was running for his life from the car, Strong was able to fire a couple of shots at him. Fortunately, neither connected.

As Land was running for his life, a car traveling in the opposite direction approached him. Charley must have had a guardian angel sitting on his shoulder because the approaching car had a Good Samaritan couple in control of it. Seeing this wild man running at them from down the road would have been sufficient for most people to hit the accelerator as they made sure that their doors were locked. But this car had a couple in it who took seriously their religious and civic responsibility to help those in need of it.

And boy, was Charley Land ever in need of some help! The man and his wife stopped their car, and Land jumped in the back seat quicker than a West Texas jack rabbit. I would have said faster than an illegal immigrant swimming across the Rio Grande from Juarez to El Paso, but that would be insensitive. And away they went, right toward John David Strong, who had commandeered Land's car as his escape vehicle.

That guardian angel was still sitting on Land's shoulder, because the first car down the road was a patrol vehicle driven by one of Leeds's finest. After a quick stop and a hasty explanation of what was going down, the cop took off after Strong with siren blaring and blue light flashing. After a brief chase, Strong lost control of Land's car and ended up about twenty yards from the road. He got out with the gun by his side, ready for action. But the patrol officer already had his duty gun pointed directly at Strong's mid-section. After a second or two of deliberation, the would-be hit man paid heed to the old maxim that discretion really is the better part of valor and dropped his pistol. No doubt an excellent move on his part since the patrol officer was renowned for his accuracy with his police issue pistol, and there is little question that he would have shot Strong graveyard dead should the would-be hit man so much as twitched.

After Strong was booked into the county lockup, events and people really just began to get interesting. First was the matter of the contents of the paper bag that Strong had retrieved from the back yard of the residence in Homewood. In addition to the pistol that Strong had pulled from the bag and had used in his attempt to murder Land, and which had been confiscated by the Leeds patrol officer after he got the drop on Strong – there were several other items of interest. Included among those items was a bottle of whisky, a woman's dress, lipstick and other make-up accouterments and some Benzedrine tablets. As Slim Pickens, playing Major "King" Cong, said in Stanley Kubric's classic *Dr. Strangelove*: "A feller could have a pretty good weekend in 'Vegas with that stuff."

John David Strong, as weird a duck as I ever dealt with in the criminal justice system, had no intentions of using these items in Vegas. As we later learned, he intended to kill Land, put the dress and makeup on the corpse after pouring the whisky all over him and then dumping the body near the Rage, a gay nightclub on Birmingham's Southside, making it appear that Land had been living a secret life and was just another gay victim being killed by a lover or by a gay basher. I guess the Benzedrine was for Strong so that he could stay awake while executing his murderous plan. Regardless of what he intended for the Benzedrine, it was recovered by the police along with the other items in the sack.

One item was recovered from Strong's person – either from his wallet or simply stuck in his pocket – that opened the way for the months-long investigation that resulted in the indictment and arrest of Larry Steven Kimbrough, business partner of Charles Land. Although he didn't know it at the time, John David Strong's failure to remove this piece of paper with a telephone number on it proved to be the luckiest mistake that he probably ever had made in his long career as a professional criminal. In a strange twist of irony, that piece of paper with the telephone number on it saved him from the certainty of a life sentence without parole, and instead substituted a meager forty year sentence with the possibility– however unlikely – of parole. The piece of paper? Oh, it just had Larry Steven Kimbrough's home telephone number on it. And Strong was cooperative enough to have made numerous long-distance calls to that number from Montgomery, using a telephone from the house where he was staying in a rented room.

Enter one of my all time favorite people and investigators, Detective Sergeant Tony Hudson of the Leeds Police Department. Tony recently retired as the Chief of the Leeds PD and I was honored to attend his retirement reception. I have rarely, if ever, worked with a better detective or person than Tony. And I was lucky to have him working this case or we never would have gotten an indictment, much less a conviction, of Mr. Kimbrough.

One of the first investigative steps taken by Hudson was a trip to Montgomery to the rooming house where John David Strong rented a room from the owner, some old coot who used to belong to the Klan and made no effort to hide his membership. That fact alone caused us to investigate him for any possible connection to the attempted hit on Charles Land. But there was no connection, just some burned-out old racist who picked up a few extra bucks renting out one of the rooms of his house. Strong had moved out shortly before his attempted hit on Land, but fortunately he had unwittingly supplied us with the key to the connection between him and Kimbrough.

Going through some discarded papers that Strong had tossed in a waste basket, Tony found a magazine that caught his attention. And that magazine was *Soldier of Fortune*. Being the good, curious investigator that he was, Sgt. Hudson turned to the classified personal ads that he knew would be in the back of the magazine. The personal ad that proved to be the connection just about jumped off the page and smacked Hudson upside his head. There it was, circled by Strong, who never imagined that anybody but himself would see it: a personal ad with Larry Kimbrough's home telephone number and a P.O. Box in Palmerdale, Alabama, a small municipality just outside Birmingham where Kimbrough lived.

Soldier of Fortune was already being sued by the relatives of an individual who was the victim of someone who responded to a personal ad in the magazine that was a thinly veiled recruitment ad for a hit man. The respondent to the ad was hired and did the deed. The incident was reported by a wire service and carried by newspapers across the country. Evidently, Kimbrough either read about the lawsuit or heard, by word of mouth from whatever group of thugs he counted as friends, about using the personals section of *Soldier of Fortune* as a means to locate a hit man.

And thus, a marriage of convenience was born – Larry Steven Kimbrough, the front man in a business venture, who was too lazy, too greedy and just plain immoral that he would prefer to make his money by murdering his business partner instead of playing by the rules, and John David Strong, the parolee willing to kill if the price was right. It definitely was not a marriage made in heaven. But Kimbrough viewed it as a means for gaining his notion of heaven on earth – the $1million in life insurance proceeds that he would receive as beneficiary of the "key man" policy designating Poor Charles Land as the insured, should Land meet the Grim Reaper. And John David Strong was the Reaper.

Kimbrough was thoughtful enough to pay for a personal ad in SOF (*Soldier of Fortune*) magazine where someone with that kind of sociopathic personality might read it and make inquiry by telephone to the number listed in the solicitation, in this case, Kimbrough's home number. Now Kimbrough may have been one evil SOB, but he wasn't stupid. The solicitation ad was cryptic in certain aspects, reading almost as if Kimbrough was looking for a few adventurous types seeking money and notoriety by engaging in some unspecified but challenging and dangerous activity. Either that or it read almost as if Kimbrough was holding himself out as some sort of swash-buckler looking for adventure. Regardless of how it was worded, it was sufficient to prompt John David Strong to reach out and touch Kimbrough, so to speak. And in the spring or early summer of 1985, he did. A deal was struck with Strong agreeing to kill Charley Land for filthy lucre, a.k.a "blood money."

There followed a series of telephone calls from Kimbrough's number to Strong's, which left a paper trail of corroboration between the two conspirators. But all of these threads of evidence meant nothing without someone to weave them together in a cloth that completed the picture. And John David Strong became the weaver. As I wrote earlier, Strong was one of the weirdest ducks ever to quack in a pond. He looked like G. Gordon Liddy and sounded like the Shadow's stepson. He also was a viper with fangs like spikes, and was a living example of why prosecutors should handle cooper-ating witnesses ("snitches") with Kevlar gloves. More about that lesson in snake handling later. For now, I'll simply mix my metaphors and state the obvious: a snake never changes its spots (or a leopard its skin.)

For weeks following Strong's arrest, Hudson and I worked hard-er than a month-old biscuit without the yeast, putting together a case against Kimbrough that reflected those long hours, late nights and stale coffee. We had to put together a case that withstood any attack because our only witness who could put the hat right on Kim-brough's head was none other than John David Strong.

As long as he cooperated, Tony and I ultimately believed that we had enough evidence to convict Kimbrough. The balance of our evidence was circumstantial, but strongly corroborative of what Strong was telling us about his agreement with Kimbrough, and his subsequent attempt to kill Charley Land. And Strong cooperated in a more-than-satisfactory manner, at least until the night before closing arguments. And then he tried to eat his cake and have it too. He kept his part of the bargain with us in his testimony, but shortly thereafter attempted to avoid the snitch jacket that he would surely wear in the big house. Before going into his treachery, his deal was that, in exchange for his complete cooperation and truthful testimony, he would plead guilty to an offense that would avoid the Alabama Habitual Felony Offender Act mandatory sentence of life without parole.

He was promised that if he entered a guilty plea to attempted assault in the first degree, a "B" felony, the State would recommend a sentence of 40 years, but with the possibility of parole. He was in his 50's at the time, but at least he had a chance, albeit a slim one, to one day walk out of prison rather than be carried out, in a pine box. And so he spilled his guts about Kimbrough and his plan to get rich through the proceeds of the "key man" life insurance policy. However, he later tried to weasel out of his testimony in a fashion to be described shortly.

Kimbrough was allowed to remain a free man until Hudson and I had squeezed the evidentiary fruit as dry as we could get it, which included the would-be hit man, John David Strong. We also matched up as much corroborating evidence as we could with the weird and deadly scheme of Mr. "I could work for a living, but I'd rather kill my business partner" Larry Steven Kimbrough. Strong was designated to do the heavy lifting in executing Kimbrough's blueprint for murder. The key to the whole puzzle, obviously, was Strong, he of the lengthy criminal history and the G.Gordon Liddy looks. Not the kind of individual that prosecutors like to put on the stand to prove their case, but you take 'em as you find 'em.

Sometimes you just have to swallow hard, and play the cards that you hold. Either that or you throw in and cut your losses. We played and played big, believing that truth, justice and the American way would prevail. Or at least that those laudable objectives would give us a fighting chance, one in which total commitment would result, if not in glorious victory, at least a result which would leave us with a minimum of egg on our faces. Were we afraid of falling short of the goal and embarrassing ourselves and our bosses? Hell, yes! And that's probably the main reason that we worked our law enforcement asses off in gathering every scintilla of evidence and information that we could dig up about Kimbrough and anybody associated with him.

Detective Sergeant Tony Hudson and I became absolutely ubiquitous during the course of the next several months in our search for evidentiary ties between Strong and Kimbrough. And we continued showing up in rumored haunts of Kimbrough's until just before trial time. We had made the decision to take the case directly to the grand jury, thus avoiding a preliminary hearing and Sheffield's opportunity to try to punch holes in our case before we got it off the ground. This decision also cut the time factor to trial by about three months – the approximate interval between a preliminary hearing and grand jury presentation.

When the grand jury returned a true bill of indictment, charging Kimbrough with one count of solicitation to commit murder, Hudson and I were given the warrant by the judge, and we made a very hurried trip to Kimbrough's residence in order to serve the warrant and place the little scoundrel under arrest. It was a good thing that we acted when we did since Kimbrough and his wife were packing to move to Virginia. Not having to fight an extradition battle meant that we saved time and energy, as well as the legal process in another state where Kimbrough's rich father-in-law held sway and influence. Hudson and I went to his house to arrest him the evening of the same night that the grand jury returned the indictment. When we arrived at his house, we observed the For Sale sign in the front yard and then discovered Kimbrough and his wife in the midst of packing their belongings. The posse had arrived just in time to nab the bad guy before he could disappear into the sunset.

We went to the Kimbrough residence, and when he opened the door in response to our knock, recited his rights to him and explained the situation to him and his wife. Before we were able to spirit him off in the darkness to a Sheriff's Department substation for a little friendly interview, Sweet Thing had called her daddy in Virginia. He was most definitely *not* a gentleman. He informed me that he was going to notify the United States Attorney in my district, apparently for having the gall and temerity to have obtained a grand jury indictment of his son-in-law. I supplied him with Frank Donaldson's name and invited him to please call Mr. Donaldson.

Whether he contacted the head fed, I don't know, but I do know that Mr. Donaldson hired me several years later to do in federal court what I had been doing in state court for a number of years – ride herd on the bad guys and send them off to the slammer for lengthy stretches of time to contemplate their misdeeds while developing a real aversion to taking showers. Kimbrough's daddy-in-law apparently didn't swing much weight in the hinterlands of North Alabama, be it Birmingham or Sand Mountain for all that I knew.

About two months later, Hudson and I were still gathering little nuggets, morsels and tidbits of evidence that could be consumed by twelve hungry jurors and one no-nonsense judge at the feast of justice when the meal was ready to be served up to them. The case had received more than the usual paragraph of printer's ink the week before a jury was selected once we finally lit the candle and achieved successful lift-off. By that time I believed that Hudson and I were as well prepared as time and hard work would allow.

And the trial that followed demonstrated exactly how hard we had worked putting it together. I was more than ably assisted at that trial by my old friend from Judge Pearson's courtroom, Bob Posey. The star witness for the state of course, was that redoubtable thug turned rat, John David Strong. Everyone in the courtroom sat up and took notice when I called Strong to the stand. My direct examination of him was compelling and brought out all of the weird details of his plan as the hireling of Larry Steven Kimbrough to murder Charles Land. But, of course, the acid test of how the jury would assess him as a witness would be how well he could handle the expected tsunami of cross-examination triggered by Hurricane Larry.

The interested parties and the courthouse hangers on who came to see a good show, all had been waiting for this confrontation since the jury was struck. Larry Sheffield, Jr., the old man himself, the Lone Wolf, in addition to all of his wiles, tricks of the trade and just plain damned good advocacy, was renowned as perhaps the best cross-examiner of government snitches as anyone who had ever strapped on the firearm of the trial lawyer with bad intentions. Surely he would grievously wound, if not outright kill, the prosecution's instrument for connecting all of the dots of circumstantial evidence and would leave the State's case on life support.

But a funny thing happened on the way to the execution. Nobody had given Strong a copy of the script, particularly the part where Sheffield reduces him to a quivering mass of lies, half- truths and fear of the master cross examiner himself. In fact, as much as Sheffield sneeringly tried to depict Strong as a very clever liar who was trying to frame his client for a good deal from the prosecutor, the more Strong seemed to enjoy the proceedings and actually told Sheffield "more power to you" in his efforts.

Far from being intimidated by this acknowledged master of the courtroom, Strong actually seemed amused. This type of reaction to an opposing attorney on cross examination normally doesn't endear the witness to the jury, but in Strong's case it worked like a charm. Not that anyone in the courtroom mistook him for anything other than the cold-blooded, albeit incompetent would be assassin, which he was in fact. But he was so totally relaxed and candid that he came across as credible to the jury. Sheffield finished his cross-examination of Strong without drawing blood, and I wisely chose not to try to smooth out a very few rough edges on redirect. Strong was excused as a witness, taken back to his cage, and I believed that the only other time that I would be hearing his name would be in closing arguments. Boy, was I ever wrong! And I would soon find out exactly what a double dealing rat John David Strong actually was.

The remainder of the trial went down just as smooth as a baby's butt after a warm bath and a talcum powder rub. We put a witness on the stand that just a few days before the attempted hit placed Kimbrough at his gun shop purchasing the bullets for the gun that Strong used in his attempt on Land's life. The only item of significance that we missed was locating from whom or where Kimbrough had gotten the gun that he had given to Strong to use as the murder weapon. But Sheffield didn't know that. Kimbrough had told him where he had gotten it and told Sheffield that he gave it to Strong merely to protect himself.

Sheffield was far too seasoned a criminal defense attorney to buy into that lie, but I'm certain that he gave Kimbrough the "talk" prior to interviewing him. It is unethical for an attorney to put a witness on the stand with knowledge that the witness will perjure himself. Thus, the "talk". Inherent in the "talk" are two elements: (1) You are my client, and I will believe what you tell me. (2) Tell me whatever incriminating evidence is out there, and either don't provide any explanation for its existence, or make sure that whatever reason you tell me is at least plausible. This process is a useful fiction for a defense attorney to rely on and still say with a straight face that he didn't "know" that his witness was going to commit perjury. And who *really* can say with absolute, 100-percent certainty that whatever nonsense is being spouted by the witness really isn't factually correct? Such goings on allow defense attorneys to maintain a semblance of integrity, at least in their own minds.

And it is precisely this sort of slick "trickerization" (legal terminology for lying) that turns ordinary citizens who aren't lawyers into raging, foaming-at-the-mouth haters of lawyers. That is, until they get drunk at the office Christmas party, and while driving home with a blood-alcohol reading of about 1.8, run over some grandmother crossing the street with an armful of Christmas presents purchased at Wal-Mart for her fourteen grand-children.

And *that's* when they suddenly begin to appreciate the fine art of telling your lawyer some utterly absurd story of how the car was actually being driven by your evil (not to mention non-existent) twin, from whom you were separated at birth, who miraculously found you that very night, but car-jacked you and then disappeared into the mists, leaving you to take the fall. Who's to say that scenario didn't *really* happen? Certainly not your lawyer. And now your lawyer may call you as a witness with a clear conscience, or at least what passes for one in the criminal defense bar.

And so, the defendant himself, the far-less-than-honorable Larry Steven Kimbrough, took the stand to testify on his own behalf. It was delicious. Sheffield took him through his paces, having Kimbrough provide at least semi-plausible explanations for all of the telephone calls, the scrap of paper in Strong's pocket with Kimbrough's telephone number on it, and all of the other evidence that the State had introduced tying Strong to Kimbrough, including the ad which Kimbrough had placed in *Soldier of Fortune* magazine which had been found by Tony Hudson in the waste basket of Strong's room at the residence in Montgomery. You remember that ad, don't you? It was the one with Kimbrough's home telephone number on it and read like a recruiting poster for would-be hit men. But there was one very important item that we had but couldn't tie to Kimbrough, the gun that Strong used in his attempt on Charles Land's life. Yes, we ran every gun trace known to man at that time, but kept rolling snake eyes.

The one thing that we neglected to do was to check the classified ads in the Birmingham News in the weeks preceding the attempted hit. Had we done so, we would have been able to locate the source of the heater that Strong unsuccessfully used in his ill-fated attempt to eliminate Land. Of course, Sheffield didn't have that problem; all that he did was to ask Kimbrough how he came into possession of the weapon that had changed hands, both legally and illegally, so many times that it became impossible to trace. He never would have asked him that question if he knew for a fact that we had not located or identified the source of that weapon. And so, rather than take the chance that we had located the man who placed the ad in the paper the week prior to the hit gone bad, Sheffield called Kimbrough to the stand and Larry the K had to "eat the evidence" as we say in the trade.

Because, you see, had Kimbrough taken the stand and testified that he knew nothing about the gun, he faced the very real possibility of the State calling to the witness stand as a rebuttal witness the actual seller of the firearm. Of course, we couldn't have done that because we had not read the classified ads in the Sunday paper one week prior to the attempted murder. But we had been so omnipresent in the months preceding the trial, the old Lone Wolf couldn't risk the possibility of what I just described occurring at trial.

Of course, although Sheffield never instructed his client to lie under oath, I'm certain that in an extended version of the "talk," he merely pointed out to Kimbrough that if Kimbrough testified and denied knowing about the gun, and if we had indeed located the seller, we could call the seller as a rebuttal witness, and any slim chance of an acquittal would have approximately the same chance of occurring as the Wicked Witch of the East would have of winning the title of Miss Congeniality in the Miss America contest. And thus, Kimbrough would have to come up with a plausible explanation for why he had purchased the Roscoe and how it had come to be in Strong's possession as the instrument used by Strong in his unsuccessful attempt to snuff poor Charley Land. "Rotsa ruck," Mr. Kimbrough!

During the course of our investigation, Hudson and I had come to know Kimbrough probably better than he knew himself. Several weeks prior to the trial, we had been interviewing the other members of the business venture who numbered no more than a handful. One of these folks was a secretary, fairly attractive and a very pleasant person. To avoid any possibility of identifying her, I'll simply call her "Sue Ann." I was interviewing her in one room while Hudson was talking with another member of the venture in a different room. By the time of the interview, I learned that Kimbrough had once been caught by his wife in Houston, Texas cheating on her with some local floozy. I also strongly believed that he was, or had been, cheating on the little woman with some Birmingham version of the Texas Jezebel, but I never could prove it until I interviewed Sue Ann.

An interesting thing happened during my interview with Sue Ann. As I was observing her, it suddenly hit me as to what Kimbrough, based on his total lack of morals, must have done. I interrupted Sue Ann, and looking her straight in the eye, I asked her whether she had ever slept with Kimbrough. She cast her eyes down as her face flushed and tears began to form, even as she tried to maintain a semblance of composure and dignity. She admitted that she had done so, and on several occasions. I asked her whether her husband knew, and she said yes, that she had told him. My incredulous response was: "Why did you tell your husband?" She replied, "Because I thought that you already knew, and that it was going to come out." Hudson and I apparently had successfully created an image of two gumshoes that would leave no stone unturned in a relentless search for the truth. This, when you think about it, was a pretty accurate assessment of us and our investigation.

The circumstances of their several encounters all were a product of extortion. Kimbrough told Sue Ann that if she did not sleep with him, he would fire her. What a prince of a fellow! And since she and her husband were already struggling just to pay their rent, she gave in to the little rat (with apologies to all other rodents) on several occasions. But, such information would have been irrelevant and inadmissible, barring some blunder by Sheffield in the nature of somehow injecting Kimbrough's character into evidence. During Sheffield's cross examination of Sue Ann, he unwittingly opened the door about as wide as the rear end of the circus fat lady. Proving once again that God *is* on the side of the angels and *does* love the police (pronounced po' lease).

I had called Sue Ann as a witness for two reasons: (1) to state certain facts about the business, and (2) to tell the jury about seeing Kimbrough one week before the attempted hit on Charley Land at a gun shop in the area where Kimbrough lived. I also had called as a witness the owner of the gun shop. He testified that he did sell the make and caliber of bullets recovered by the police from the pistol taken from Strong by the arresting officer, as well as the fact that he sold tiny zip-lock bags, precisely like the ones recovered with ammunition from Strong when he was arrested.

But this testimony, while serving as a couple of bricks in the house being built to imprison Kimbrough, was nothing compared to what I was able to get into evidence when I had the opportunity to conduct my redirect examination. Because, you see, Mr. Larry "Sleaze" Kimbrough had committed the cardinal sin of withholding damaging information about himself from his lawyers. Knowing Sheffield and son as well as I did, I knew that they would squeeze every drop of juice from Kimbrough and his sordid past, just to avoid stumbling into an area of Kimbrough's personal life that otherwise would be unavailable grist for the mill of redirect examination.

But I knew some things about the little liar's past that I was sure he withheld from his mouthpieces. So, notwithstanding Sheffield's command to his client that he wanted to know every time in Kimbrough's life that he had so much as "broken wind," lying came as naturally to Kimbrough as fighting did to a drunken Irishman. (The reader will please excuse the writer's political incorrectness, but he is half Irish and has been in a few drunken brawls in his youth.) And thus, the table was set for a repast of country-fried Kimbrough.

Prior to Kimbrough's testimony, the howitzer had to be fired by Sue Ann, but only after being primed by an unsuspecting Sheffield. Sue Ann had not caused any major damage to Kimbrough during my direct examination, save for a few dents to Kimbrough's defense in her testimony about seeing him at the gun shop the week prior to the inept attempted assassination of Charley Land by John David Strong. But the great barrister himself simply could not resist the temptation to turn the witness to his own advantage during his cross-examination of her. Thus, he of the silver hair and the dated pompadour, stepped into a pile of manure that he never saw coming in his trek across the pasture of cross-examination.

The old man had tried to get Sue Ann to say something nice about the defendant, something that might tend to demonstrate Kimbrough's humanity; even that he could be a nice guy on occasion. But a cobra is still a cobra, regardless of whether it has ever bitten anybody. And, unbeknown to Mr. Sheffield, Kimbrough had bitten Sue Ann and had gotten his poison into her bloodstream. And that poison splashed over on the jury when Kimbrough's unwitting mouthpiece asked Sweet Sue the one question that he later regretted having asked. And it was all due to his client's duplicity with him. And that question was whether Kimbrough had ever hurt her or in any way threatened her. She hesitated in her answer and Sheffield pressed her. Big mistake! She began stuttering something incomprehensible, and Sheffield moved on when he caught the drift that this area was one he did not want to enter.

But the door had been opened for my redirect examination, and I kicked it off the hinges when my opportunity came with my second turn with the witness. Whereupon, Sue Ann shamefully and tearfully admitted her several encounters with Kimbrough due to his threats to fire her if she refused his crude advances. I then asked her whether she was pregnant and whether her husband had accompanied her to court. She answered in the affirmative to both questions. She also stated unequivocally that the father-to-be of her expected child was her husband. We were able to prove the dates that she submitted to Kimbrough by producing the motel records of the Interstate Motel which was Kimbrough's choice of venues in which to engage in his dirty work.

And then Sheffield compounded his original unwitting error by attempting to shame Sue Ann before the jury, a majority of who were women. Sue Ann cried softly while answering his demeaning questions and presented a picture of a woman who had sinned and was repentant, and who wore her scarlet "A" with dignity and class. The jurors, particularly the women, loved her. And her husband, who I had Sue Ann identify in the first row, sat tall and supportive of the woman that he loved. This demonstration of mutual support and love was in sharp contrast to the actions of Kimbrough's wife who stalked out with children in tow at the first mention of her husband's infidelity. I gained an appreciation for homework that I'd never had in all my years of stumbling through school. And don't think that the jurors did not take note of the contrast between the reactions of the respective spouses.

But for a wild card in the deck that no one could have anticipated, the case was over, and all that remained was for closing arguments to be made and for the judge to instruct the jury as to the law. We broke for the evening, with arguments scheduled for 9:00 in the morning. When I returned to the courtroom the next morning, I was met by a very sober appearing Lawrence Sheffield Jr. and his son, Lawrence III. And they hit me squarely between the eyes with a situation that I had never encountered before or since during the course of a trial. In fact, I am not aware of any other lawyer to whom this has happened.

Sheffield the Elder informed me that John David Strong had called him the previous evening at his own house. I could feel the color draining from my face while my gut felt as if I had just been punched in the solar plexus by Muhammad Ali. Sheffield, smelling what was going down, referred the caller, who wouldn't identify himself by name, but whose voice could be none other than that of the hit man turned rat, JDS himself, to Sheffield III. The younger Sheffield listened carefully as Strong said that he "knew" that the guy who had rolled over on Kimbrough had perjured himself. It was a classic instance of someone trying to eat his cake and have it too. That sweet taste of impending victory began to sour in my mouth. I barely managed to avoid losing my breakfast in open court.

But, before we could proceed with, *whatever*, there was first the small matter of informing Judge Joe Jasper of the previous evening's developments which had deposited a heaping portion of very sour curd on the cream of the State's case. Judge Jasper handled this curve ball with his usual equanimity. He informed us that he would allow the defense to reopen its case and allow Sheffield the Younger to testify if he so desired. Of course, he wanted to testify about the previous evening's strange call from the even stranger would be hit man, John David Strong.

And that's the way this showpiece of weird judicial events and weirder human behavior unfolded. The old man called his son as a witness who told the jury about the telephone call from, and conversation with, the-not-so-mysterious stranger the previous night. Although the caller didn't identify himself, not a single person who heard young Sheffield testify doubted that the caller was John David Strong. On cross-examination, I didn't ask a single question. What would have been the point, other than giving Sheffield the opportunity to hammer home what the jury already believed, namely that John David Strong was attempting to play both ends toward the middle.

Long before Kimbrough's trial I had learned the first rule of cross-examination: Don't! Adherence to that rule served me well on that occasion. The potentially devastating testimony didn't even scratch the skin of my case. And I underscored its being punctured like a cheap balloon in my closing argument by referring to the Sheffields as "honorable men" who wouldn't stretch what Strong had said, even at the cost of losing a trial (and what had to be a very large fee.) The old man never did forgive me for referring to him as an "honorable man." He told me after the jury had convicted his client that hearing my reference in open court caused him to feel the knife as I plunged it between his ribs and deep into his back.

Closing arguments were almost anti-climactic, given the strength of the case that Tony Hudson had built and that I had presented to the jury. The members of that group of citizens returned a guilty verdict in less than an hour. The next day, Sheffield the Elder paid Hudson and me a great compliment by taking the trouble to stop by my boss's office and tell him that the case that we had put on was the best-prepared case that he had seen in more than thirty years of practicing law. David Barber, my boss, related those remarks to me later that day. It felt good, and I had established myself throughout the legal community of Jefferson County as a force with which to be reckoned.

And Larry Steven Kimbrough would be a guest of the Alabama penal system for years to come.

Chapter Six

A Few That I Remember

You've met the people, been in the courtrooms and heard the tall tales, which just happened to be true. I now will introduce you to a few of the most unforgettable lawyers and other individuals who just happened to make an indelible mark on my memory, and some who seared my very soul. Some of these people and vignettes I have made reference to in the preceding pages, while some I haven't previously mentioned. Perhaps this chapter of the book will serve as a detailed topographical layout of both my years as a state prosecutor as well as a narrative –blemishes and beauty marks alike – of what occurs every day in the courtrooms of our country.

One of the most unforgettable and charmingly corrupt, persons that I ever met – as well as being a bullying judicial tyrant – was the late, but hardly lamented, Jefferson County District Court Judge Jack Montgomery, mentioned about briefly earlier in these recollections. He has already been the subject of at least one book, Jack's Law, written by former *Birmingham News* reporter Steve Joynt. I mention Montgomery only in passing for a number of reasons, chief of which is that I don't have enough time in this book to do justice to all of the injustices perpetrated by the black-robed scoundrel.

If I write a book about my years as a federal prosecutor, I will provide the reader with much more detail. Until that time I will merely mention another judge whose role in unmasking and unseating Montgomery has heretofore not been made public. Alabama District Court Judge Bob Cahill, now retired, is an unsung hero in the whole sordid tale. I will say simply that Judge Cahill smelled a conniving rat named Jack and knew enough as a former prosecutor to set the wheels of justice in motion after then Officer Mark Hobbs of the Hoover Police Department went to him one night seeking help. After listening to what Hobbs had to say, the good judge sent Hobbs to my house, knowing that I would not only know *what* to do, but *how* to go about doing it.

Hobbs and his partner came over to my house and told me the whole sorry mess. I immediately contacted Special Agent Steve Brannan of the FBI, gave him a quick and brief heads up as to what was going on and then put Hobbs on the 'phone. Within half an hour, Hobbs had his marching orders and about a year and a half later Montgomery entered a plea of guilty. Sentencing was deferred for several weeks, but the old reprobate cheated the hangman by killing himself two days before he was to be sentenced.

Mark Hobbs deservedly was looked upon by both law enforcement and the people of Jefferson County as a hero. But Judge Cahill deserves both recognition and a sincere "thank you" from the general public. I am proud to say that both of these men are among my friends as well as being the best kind of public servants.

I have had the opportunity of working with some of the most conscientious and skilled prosecutors practicing their craft in the country. I have referred to many of them in this manuscript, particularly the entire staff in Mobile. Don Beebe, who I worked with in the Port City, was as gifted a trial attorney as I have ever seen. Tom Harrison was both talented as well as fearless. Gloria Bedwell was absolutely tenacious and didn't know the meaning of "quit." And Lloyd Copeland was both flamboyant as well as scholarly. Also, Joe Thetford and Bill Steele were rock solid and projected both credibility and confidence to a jury. In fact, we probably had the best group of prosecutors in any District Attorney's office in Alabama.

But several that I worked with in Jefferson County were at the least their equals. Three from the District Attorney's Office stand out, and several more from the United States Attorneys Office, but I'll withhold my praise for them until I write about my years as a federal prosecutor. But, back to the trio for the best I saw in a state court, and in no particular order, were Teresa Tanner Pulliam, George Andrews and Roger Brown. Teresa and I had worked together for about a year in Mobile and then, following her marriage in Birmingham, for more than three years in Jefferson County.

George was very intelligent, a very able writer and researcher, and was possessed of the ability to "paint the story" for the jury better than any prosecutor I've ever seen try a case. George was the son of a Congressman who was one of only two Alabama Democratic Representatives who had survived the Goldwater effect in 1964 which was the first crack in the dam of the once "Solid South." The other Democratic survivor was Armistead Selden, whose son Jack was a law school classmate of mine as well as being my boss for a period of time, having been appointed by George Herbert Walker Bush to serve as the United States Attorney for the Northern District of Alabama. But I digress.

Roger Brown was our chief deputy, having returned to the DA's office after several years as a criminal defense attorney. He had worked as a deputy district attorney in that office in the early 1970s. Some might say that the prodigal son had returned, but the people of Jefferson County were the real beneficiaries of his return to the

District Attorney's Office. Roger was one of the best criminal defense attorneys in the state. I would much prefer to try a case *with* him rather than against him.

He was also a Jesuit-trained graduate of Georgetown University, and that training and education by the members of the Order of Jesus served him well as a prosecutor. He had a steel trap mind and an ability to identify the issues in a case as well as any prosecutor I knew. He also had a gift as a debater which crossed over to his facility for making cogent arguments to a jury in terms that they could understand. Roger Brown, arguably was the best prosecutor I have ever known.

Teresa Pulliam, now a state court circuit Judge, is several years younger than I am. As I mentioned earlier in the book, Teresa started out in the Mobile District Attorney's Office, several months after I began working there. In fact, I gave her the first jury case that she tried, with all of about one hour to prepare for it. She was not found wanting in the courtroom and within a year had established herself as the reigning queen of Mobile Circuit Court. After another couple of years in Mobile, she married Max Pulliam, a Birmingham attorney, and subsequently moved to that city and secured a job with the Jefferson County District Attorney's Office where I had established myself after a period of perhaps two years. I loved the fact that once again we would be working together, doing something that we both loved doing. I had the pleasure watching Teresa continue her development as an advocate while we worked together in the Jefferson County District Attorney's Office. In trial, she was the absolute best at finding the acceptable mix of personal passion with dispassionate objectivity that there was – bar none. And she had a near insatiable drive to win – and win by the rules, such was her respect for our profession. Teresa, when at her best in trial, was as good as prosecutors come.

George Andrews, Son of the South, and a thoroughly engaging raconteur, began work on January 3, 1985. That day was also my first on the job, and we met as we were walking to the courthouse from the lot where we parked our cars. It was a bitter cold day, and the wind was cutting right through us, but we managed to stay distracted by talking about what lay ahead for us. Also with us was Paul Greene, who himself was a new hire from the Morgan County District Attorney's Office. The three of us would become close friends, although Paul was with us for only about a year before he was hired as an Assistant United States Attorney and, after establishing himself in that office, was appointed by the District Court Judges to the position of United States Magistrate. He worked in the federal courthouse a few blocks from our little nest in the county courthouse.

I wrote earlier that George was the son of a deceased former Democratic Congressman. He had himself been a Congressional page in Washington at one point during his father's tenure. During the early part of his career as a lawyer he had been a deputy district attorney in the Bessemer Division of Jefferson County, had been in private practice for a few years after that, and then decided to become a prosecutor again. George was marvelous with a jury and an expert in cross-examining a witness. And besides his considerable oratorical skills, he was intelligent and a real student and scholar of the law.

Roger Brown was four years older than I was, but after graduating from Georgetown, he went directly to Cumberland School of Law in Birmingham, and, upon graduating and passing the bar examination, immediately began work as a prosecutor in the District

Attorney's Office. Thus, he became a trial lawyer about twelve or so years before I did. Roger established himself in the early 1970s as one tough prosecutor during his first tenure with the D.A.'s office, which was only for two or three years, and then as a criminal defense attorney until he found Jesus and left the dark side, returning to the District Attorney's Office about 1986 to do the Lord's work. He not only was a top-notch litigator but was also about as mean a prosecutor who ever walked the floors of the Jefferson County Courthouse. And that assessment is made only in the most complimentary fashion.

I had tried – or would in the future try – cases both with and against each member of this trio, all three having been in, or ultimately going into the private sector. Needless to say, although I remain close friends with each one of the triumvirate, it was easier to like them when we all were prosecutors. Fortunately, the vast majority of our trial work consisted of working as teammates rather than adversaries.

But earning a guilty verdict as a prosecutor normally is easier to obtain than it is for a defense attorney to earn a verdict of not guilty for his client. This expected outcome is the norm, despite the higher burden of proof carried by the prosecutor into every trial. In fact, the only reason that a prosecutor ever should receive a verdict of not guilty should be either a fluke, a "dog" of a case or simply by being "out-lawyered." Too many not guilty verdicts and the prosecutor should begin looking for another line of work. Of course there are a few rare instances of a defendant being innocent, at least of the indicted charge. We in the prosecutorial arm of the judicial system refer to innocent individuals being charged as a "statistical anomaly."

But during those years when George, Teresa, Roger and I were all on the same team, we generally kicked the defense bar's individual and collective rear ends and had a great time doing it. I prosecuted and/or assisted in the investigations of more than a few of the highest profile cases that occurred during this time period. Some I tried myself, but often with one of the prosecutors just mentioned. And still others I tried with another of the prosecutors in the office. In fact, one of my all time favorite people, as well as being a personal favorite of mine as a trial partner, was a brush headed pit bull named Mike Anderton. He was, and is, a goody. But this trio was special, and had the added benefit of being very good.

THE CRESTWOOD RAPIST

TERESA AND I TRIED or prepared any number of very high profile cases. One was that of Ryan Darden, aka the Crestwood Rapist. This poster boy for violent sexual offenses against women raped more than twenty elderly women during a two-year period of time in the Crestwood neighborhood of Birmingham. The first happened to be living alone near Darden's home, but she didn't know him. As his victim list got longer, he was becoming more and more violent, beating up and robbing the women. And if their husbands happened to be at home, he would beat them up and make them watch him rape their wives. It was only a matter of time, in my opinion, before this serial rapist became a serial murderer.

Through some excellent police work, Ryan Darden finally was taken into custody in the summer of 1987. Although there was overwhelming evidence against him, race reared its ugly head as it often does in criminal cases, and convicting him became problematic. The defendant was young, handsome, a college football player and black. All of his victims were older and, save for the first one, white. The result was a smoldering community of people who had been the real, and sometimes imagined, victims of all the Ella Mae Ewells pointing the finger of guilt at all of the Tom Robinsons unlucky enough to be the scapegoat of a white woman too fearful to admit that she had seduced him. In this case, even though the defense never tried to argue consensual sex, the old bugaboo of black men being wrong-fully accused of raping white women had asserted itself shortly af-ter Darden's arrest, even though statistically such events are next to nothing compared to the number of white men raping white women and being prosecuted for it.

As the trial drew closer, some members of the black community were taking up money to help pay for Darden's defense. And senti-ment for him continued to grow right up to jury selection.

Teresa and I had made a tactical decision in the weeks preceding the trial in order to dilute, if not entirely eliminate, any pressure on the jurors to acquit Darden because of his race. Instead of filing a motion with the Court to join all of the offenses for trial, which like-ly would have been granted because of the similarity of the crimes and evidence, we elected to try only the first assault, the rape of the only black woman in the entire group of more than twenty victims.

Our strategy worked, and it worked for several reasons. Our vic-tim was the sweetest old lady you can imagine and she was a strong and steadfast witness. Any attempt by the defense to portray her as some sort of neighborhood seductress was doomed from the start. The forensic evidence was strong, and we had about five strong black men on the jury who would not have hesitated to render a verdict of not guilty should the State have a weak case. Nor would they be likely to hold the State to a higher burden of proof than that required by law because of bias or some perceived feeling in much of the black community that Darden was being railroaded by a system of justice which historically had not been sympathetic to young black males. Ryan Darden, the Crestwood Rapist, was convicted by the jury that heard the case, which was characterized by the overwhelming evidence presented by the State.

One such highlight was a physical showing of an area of the defendant's chest which was white in color and shaped in a particular fashion. Mr. Darden had a condition known as vitiligo, a skin condition some African Americans have and which is characterized by a loss of pigmentation in those areas of the skin it affects.

During the course of the trial, I moved the court to order Darden to remove his shirt to see whether he had the mark described by the victim in the initial police report as well as in her testimony at trial. Of course, the defendant's attorney went ballistic in the presence of the jury, (a reaction which does nothing but help the prosecution) basing his objection on the grounds that his client would be forced to incriminate himself contrary to the protections afforded him by the Fifth Amendment to the United States Constitution. And, of course the protections afforded by that Amendment do not extend beyond the bounds of actual testimony. Courts have held for many decades that a physical showing is not testimonial in nature. Mr. Darden was then ordered by trial Judge Garrett to remove his shirt in the presence of the jury and to display his chest. When he did, you could see the faces of most of the jurors nodding in agreement with the victim and the prosecution. When the jury began their deliberations, not many people expected those deliberations to be more than a couple of hours before they reached a verdict of guilty. And that's pretty much how it all went down.

Darden and his attorneys the waived his right to a jury trial and elected to have the other cases joined for a bench trial. The judge hearing the evidence found him guilty and sentenced him accordingly. Darden is now serving multiple life sentences and likely will never be released. The women of Birmingham are at least marginally safer because of Darden's absence from the streets.

THE "DREAMER" WAS A KILLER

AND THEN THERE WAS the strange case of Tommy Bradley, the man who convicted himself. I worked with Teresa and George Andrews on this fascinating case in which a beautiful young blond woman's nude body was found in a dry creek bed by a jogger out on an early run one beautiful summer morning in 1987. She had been stabbed numerous times in the chest, and apparently her dead body had been thrown from the bridge sometime the previous night.

Her name was Tracy Schoettlin and she was taking time off from law school and working at a nice restaurant on Birmingham's Southside. Before the fall of 1987, it appeared that she might be Birmingham's very own Black Dahlia. Rarely has a crime in this area been as thoroughly investigated as the murder of Tracy Schoettlin with so little to show in the way of a solid suspect until the killer himself appeared at the sheriff's station with two lawyers in tow.

But before that day, actually the day that Tracy's body was found, David Barber summoned George, Teresa and me to his office. He told us to coordinate our efforts with the detectives with the Jefferson County Sheriff's Department and any other police agency participating in the investigation in order to be prepared for trial when a defendant was arrested. Teresa and George were given the order to try the case and I was to assist them and the investigators in locating evidence, interviewing potential suspects/witnesses and otherwise trying to figure out whodunit. At that time everyone expected a fairly quick arrest, given the evidence gathered on the day that Tracy's body was found by the jogger as well as the massive amounts of manpower being devoted to finding the murderer.

Identifying the killer, however, proved to be much more difficult than any of us imagined. This beautiful young woman who seemed to have everything going for her might just pass into the annals of crime in Birmingham as just another victim whose murderer would go uncaught and whose slaying would go unavenged. During the course of that summer, virtually the entire homicide squad of the sheriff's department conducted one of the most extensive investigations in the history of Jefferson County. Surrounding police agencies helped when called upon, and the intrepid trio from the District Attorney's Office continued working other cases as well as working hand in glove with the Sheriff's detectives. Notwithstanding the manpower and other tools available for the investigation, Tracy's killer was no closer to being identified well into the fall than on the first day of the manhunt. The case was in danger of becoming as cold as the Clintons' marriage.

Scores, perhaps hundreds, of individuals were interviewed in the summer and early fall. But aside from some personal belongings of Tracy that were found by a civilian, nothing showed up on the investigator's radar screen. Nothing, that is, until a young man named Tommy Bradley showed up at the Sheriff's station that fall accompanied by two criminal defense lawyers. We later learned that he had insisted on these two lawyers coming forward with him despite their extreme reluctance to follow his demands. Bradley said enough to the investigators to pique their interest but not enough to incriminate him. Needless to say, the sheriff's department was ready when Bradley next contacted them by telephone several weeks after he just "dropped by."

Within two or three weeks after his surprise visit to the sheriff's department, the strange person with the "Leave It To Beaver" looks and name, once again pushed himself into the spotlight of the investigation. Investigator Eddie White took the call from Bradley and listened to him for seven hours and recorded the entire conversation, all without one bathroom break. The information provided by Bradley during that diatribe constituted the bulk of the evidence used at trial to convict him, a diagnosed paranoid schizophrenic and a killer.

And it was this mental disorder that led him to the sheriff's department in his visit several weeks prior to his marathon telephone conversation with Eddie White. It seems that Bradley believed that he was being followed by the police and thus thought it necessary to make his presence known and give out some facts about the murder in order to cast suspicion away from himself. His actions betrayed the classic thinking of a paranoid personality. Until the day that he walked in with his lawyers, he was a total unknown to law enforcement. His visit aroused suspicions and his near interminable monologue on the telephone with Investigator White pretty much sealed the deal.

During the course of that recorded conversation, Bradley told White that he could "see" things, and commenced to relate to the veteran investigator what he "saw" about the murder with his psychic abilities. Bradley described certain events and items of evidence known only to the police. After weeks of transcribing the tapes, comparing and contrasting key information with scores of interviews of individuals who were either witnesses of certain events or potential suspects, and numerous conversations and meetings between investigators and prosecutors, we prepared an affidavit for a search warrant, and then presented it to a judge who, after carefully reviewing the affidavit, found that sufficient probable cause existed within the four corners of the document to meet the legal standard for issuing the search warrant that he subsequently signed. That warrant commanded law enforcement officers to search the house where Bradley lived with his parents.

Very little evidence that could be used at trial was recovered with one glaring exception. Investigators seized a personal check that they found in Bradley's bedroom. It was from an account of a young woman who had never heard of Bradley, much less met him. But she kept her check book in her mother's car. It seemed that Mom worked at a business located less than a block from a meeting place where it was believed that Bradley had attended religious services during the relevant frame of time. Earlier that summer, her car had been broken into while it was parked near the business and the meeting place. It had been vandalized – seat covers burned in a small space – in a fashion similar to what had been done to Tracy's plasticized driver's license. A citizen had found the driver's license on a street in Jefferson County several weeks after the murder.

The kicker was that the girl who owned the check lived in the same apartment complex as Tracy Schoetland, just across the street from her. Their respective parking spaces were right next to each other. It didn't take more than a dim-bulb's imagination and a modicum of logic to deduce that Tommy Bradley was the person who broke into the car and stole the check. It was likely that the young lady whose check was stolen and then recovered during the search of Bradley's bedroom was initially his intended victim.

And it was an easy step for him to locate her living quarters by looking at the address on the check, and then begin staking out her apartment. And from there, it was but a short leap to take notice of Tracey Schoettlin and switch his focus to her. That other very attractive young lady may never fully appreciate how close she came to being Bradley's victim. Also found in Bradley's house, in his bedroom, was a list of young women. Again, it was simply a matter of connecting the dots to conclude that the list contained the names of future victims. It was likely that Bradley was a serial killer in the making. It was only a fortuitous convergence of Bradley's paranoia and excellent police work that resulted in his prosecution.

And it was the prosecution of this sad combination of mental disorder and criminal acts of the murderer that led to his removal from the highways and byways of Birmingham. The evidence against Bradley, at first glance, appeared slim. But the more one studied the case which we continued building right up to trial time, the more manifest Bradley's guilt became to us. And as sure as Ted Bundy enjoyed murdering young women more than Alfred Hitchcock loved frightening movie goers, it was a dead solid certainty that Bradley, given the opportunity, would kill until he was stopped.

Teresa, George and I worked directly with the several investigators from the sheriff's department in the investigation and preparation of this case. By the time that a jury was struck, we were pasting together the final few items of evidence and testimony which would convict Bradley. Teresa and George tried the case and both were brilliant. The defendant's attorney, Bill Dawson, who had years of experience, and a well deserved reputation as one of the best criminal defense attorneys in the state, was stuck with a client who was palpably guilty and who arguably fit the legal definition of insanity, but according to the strict legal definition did not rise to the level of being insane at the time of the offense.

One anecdote is worth telling prior to moving on in this narrative. In the last frantic weeks prior to the trial, when everyone involved in the case was working full bore in preparation, Teresa was working harder than anyone, routinely staying at the office going over evidence and witness statements until 10:00 p.m. or midnight. During her meticulous preparations, she came to the belief that Tommy

Bradley's former wife might hold the key to his actions that summer. The ex, Ruthie Bradley, had already been interviewed shortly after the murder. But Teresa thought that certain bits and pieces of evidence, unknown at the time Ruthie was first interviewed, might yield some nuggets previously not discovered.

And so the great search for Ruthie began early one evening and would last until the wee hours of the next morning in an interview room of the Tarrant Police Department. Teresa was accompanied by Lt. Linn Moore of the Sheriff's Department, now deceased, but who was a terrific and tireless investigator, and a man possessed of a great and wicked sense of humor. This intrepid duo began their quest at Ruthie's last known address, but she was gone, and after checking three or four of her known hangouts without success, it became obvious that somebody at their first stop was able to contact her and that she was evading Teresa and Linn. It seemed that they were always one juke joint behind her.

Ultimately they caught up with her and she was able to recall morsels of facts and habits of her former husband which meant nothing without the context of several seemingly insignificant statements made by Tommy during the recorded seven hour conversation on the telephone with Sheriff's Investigator Eddie White months prior to Ruthie's revelations. But before Pulliam and Moore ran her to ground on the night in question, one of the places that they checked out was the Booby Trap Lounge out in the county, a former place of employment of Ruthie where she entertained the clientele with a variety of uh, "exotic dances."

Despite Teresa's vast experience in participating in other investigations and trying scores of complex cases that revealed the darkness of some men's souls, at heart she remained the nice young lady that her parents had raised her to be. She was possessed of a certain naivete' that was charming and fetching. The men in the Sheriff's Department had given her the sobriquet "Miss Scarlet," and Vivian Leigh herself would not have disagreed with this appellation. And so, she should have smelled a big, fat rat when Linn Moore told her to wait outside in the car while he "checked out" the establishment. Naturally, Miss Scarlet utterly failed to detect the large rodent that Lt. Moore was about to loose inside where she would be the recipient of its lust for unsuspecting damsels who were certain to bite the cheese after the trap was set.

After being inside for about five minutes, Linn came back outside and told Teresa that there was a gal in the back room who might be able to direct them to Ruthie. He also told her that there were a number of men at the bar, but that they were harmless and she should just smile at them and keep moving. They entered the darkened bar and walked virtually the entire length of it, navigating among a group of tables that had what appeared to be a whole team of rednecks and some pretty rough looking women accompanying a few of the coal miners, construction workers and truck drivers, all enjoying more than several cold beverages.

As Teresa passed between the tables and the bar, she could not help but to notice the number of smiles and kind words of greeting, as well as a few smirks and whispered comments concerning her "assets" emanating from the assembled pack of hungry looking male wolves. But all in all, it was not a particularly unpleasant experience for "Miss Scarlet." As she and Linn went into the back room to interview the "gal," Teresa noticed that Linn closed the door behind them and then paused for a few seconds prior to breaking into laughter. Teresa had a quizzical look on her face which gradually turned as red as her namesake when Lt. Moore let her in on the gag.

It seems that the reason she drew all of the smiles and remarks from the gentlemen in the bar was that Linn Moore had told them that he was going to be interviewing a new dancer in the back room, and that they should make her feel welcome and right at home. With that, he bolted from the back room through the bar and back to the car, leaving our heroine to fend for herself. As much as Teresa tried to stay mad at her "manager," she was still laughing an hour later.

Ultimately, that same night this relentless pair of "law dogs" snagged Ruthie in Tarrant City and took her to the Tarrant Police Department for the interview. Unlike the perfunctory interview that took place shortly after Tommy surfaced as the first real suspect, this interview had certain questions keyed to information culled from Tommy's lengthy recorded statement. And Miss Scarlet struck gold. By the time that the interview occurred at about 3:00 a.m. George Andrews had called me, rousing me from a sound sleep in my very soft bed about thirty miles away in Shelby County.

Needless to say, I drove at speeds too fast to mention in getting to Tarrant. And the rest just fell into place when trial time rolled around the next week. All of those long hours and time and attention given to seemingly insignificant details paid off in spades. The jury returned a verdict of guilty of capital murder, underscoring the difference between trying a case with only the fruits of the investigation which led to an indictment, and trying one without ever stopping the investigative process, proving once again that nothing beats solid preparation.

Most people, including Tommy Bradley, afflicted with the burden of being a paranoid schizophrenic, although "crazy as hell" in layman's terms, do not meet the test of being deemed insane as defined by the criminal code. Such a defense requires that the jury must determine whether at least one of two criteria applies before they are permitted to render a verdict of not guilty by reason of mental disease or defect, *aka "insanity."* Those two conditions are that at the time of the offense the defendant could *neither: (1) conform his behavior to the standards imposed by law, nor (2) appreciate the consequences of his actions.*

The standard question to a defense expert witness as to the first criterion is: Can you testify that the defendant would have committed this murder with a police officer standing next to him? The expert virtually always has to give the answer that the defendant *would not* have committed the murder under such conditions.

Also, as to the second criterion, the defense expert is virtually compelled to testify that the defendant understood the difference between right and wrong. And that's the hell of being a paranoid schizophrenic. You know what you are doing is wrong and you can control yourself sufficiently to not break the law in front of a police officer, but unless you've taken your medication, you will invariably find a way to commit the crime that you have in mind, because you just about *can't help yourself.* That condition was described by Robert Travers in his book Anatomy of a Murder as the "irresistible impulse" defense.

But that condition is no defense under the law in most, if not all states. In the Bradley case it would have been tantamount to an admission of guilt. Dawson was reduced to trying to defend his client by producing an "expert" witness in parapsychology that he brought in from San Francisco to testify that Bradley's "dreams" about the details of the murder and the murderer were absolutely consistent with what his research and the body of scholastic literature on the subject revealed.

After Dawson finished his direct examination of his witness we broke for lunch. I had been watching the jury during the entirety of his testimony. I suggested to George that he treat this guy with the kind of polite contempt that George could summon at the drop of a gavel. I told him to ask this charlatan just one question. George took my advice but asked two questions. The first was the standard query as to how much money the witness was being paid for his time and trouble. The second was my suggested question: "You say you're from San Francisco?" And this question was asked with that slow drawl of George's accompanied by a raised eyebrow and a meaningful glance at the jury, followed by a dismissive wave of George's hand as he began returning to counsel table and informing the Court that he had no further questions. The poor chap was totally frustrated and very likely rendered impotent. It was one of those moments that every trial attorney prays for, but too often never experiences. Bradley's "I saw it in a dream" defense was eviscerated, as was Bradley himself.

George and Teresa delivered great closing arguments and the jury returned a verdict of guilty of capital murder. They recommended a sentence of life without parole as opposed to a death verdict. The judge followed their recommendation which, in retrospect, was the appropriate sentence. Even though Bradley did not raise the insanity defense, it was obvious to anyone who watched the trial that, definition of legal sanity be damned, Tommy Bradley was one very disturbed individual, one from whom the public must be protected. Thus, justice was served in answering the most basic question of virtually any criminal trial: Is the defendant the one who "did it?" The answer, of course, was yes, and the jury got it right. But he would not be executed for his crime because the jurors accurately discerned his mental condition. And justice was served once again, this time in the punishment phase of the trial.

And Tommy Bradley to this day, goes to sleep each night with his head on a pillow paid for by the State of Alabama, in a cell designed to house and contain the worst of the worst in our fair state. And that is where he will die, because in Alabama life without parole *really means life without parole.* More than a few defendants have requested a sentence of death rather than facing decades of living in a small cage. I don't know how Mr. Bradley feels about it, but I strongly suspect that he is a totally miserable shell of a human being with a soul tortured in his lucid moments with the knowledge of what he has done. I would not be at all surprised to learn that he might now be, in a cruel twist of fate and irony, totally insane.

The "Macho Man"

ROGER BROWN WAS THE third member of this triumvirate of government paid mouthpieces (We were a quartet when I was included.) and was a razor sharp lawyer who had the added benefit when presenting his case to a jury of being as mean as a junkyard dog which hadn't been fed in a week. He could also turn off that mean streak and be as smooth as a baby's butt rubbed in mineral oil when the situation called for finesse and persuasion more than back-alley, bare-knuckle brawling.

He and I had known each other casually for years prior to working with each other. Roger was four years older than I was and also had gone directly to law school upon his matriculation at Georgetown. I had not even started law school until I was thirty years old. Thus, Roger had several years more experience than I had, but I was a quick study and relished the opportunity to try cases – the bigger, the better. Roger and I also were able to critique each others performance in trial which helped both of us the next time out of the chute.

We tried one particular murder case together and it provided some memorable opportunities to really tee off on the defendant,

Benny "Macho Man" Martin, and to enjoy the experience for years afterward. Martin was a local thug who managed to attract a number of younger thugs who thought that being around Benny enhanced what little "cool" that they thought that they had. Apparently, Benny believed that actually killing someone would enhance his stature with the members of his posse to even greater heights than those already attained by him merely by being a loudmouth drinker and petty thief.

And so he did. The soon-to-be deceased wasn't a particularly bad sort, just another mope looking for acceptance. Even a mope doesn't deserve the treatment inflicted by Benny Martin, however. Among other atrocities inflicted on the poor soul, Martin ran over this particular fellow several times with a car and then shot him to ensure that he died. Fortunately, he did it in view of witnesses, all of whom were members of his posse.

The prosecutor originally assigned to the case had taken another job just one week before the case was set for trial, and a number of witnesses had simply drifted away. Most of them were not too tied down to a particular locale, and Roger and I spent much of our pre-trial preparation just beating the bushes for them. We found one character living with his wife (girlfriend?) in a beat up old trailer located in some farmer's cow pasture in Shelby County. The inside of the trailer had dog poop on the floor along with the source of the poop and a child of about two years old crawling on the floor and playing with the puppy deposits. The dirty little urchin's father, a sad imitation of a human being, if ever there was one, was one of our key witnesses.

Shortly after Benny inflicted pain, suffering and death on the poor victim, he decided that staying in the Birmingham area would not be conducive to his long term freedom, and he fled the jurisdiction. Investigators from the sheriff's department solved the crime with dispatch and obtained a warrant for Benny's arrest. It took a few months to find him, but the "Macho Man" helped the process by breaking the law in another state and getting himself arrested – I believe in either North Dakota or Minnesota. He was extradited to Alabama after his respite up North.

But Benny just couldn't help himself; he had to boast of his foul deeds to at least one other person, in this case one Louis Blackbird, a full-blooded Sioux Indian who had at one time been a tribal policeman on his reservation. Benny should have realized that running one's mouth while in jail awaiting trial is almost tantamount to a written guarantee that he would see one of his cell mates down the road at trial time testifying against him. Perhaps he thought that he could run his mouth with impunity prior to his being extradited by Alabama. Or perhaps Benny just had to brag to somebody about what a bad ass he was.

Whatever his reason, Benny told Blackbird, who was in on assault charges, that he had been charged with murder back in Alabama, and he provided a detailed account of the crime. But he changed one element of the story, a change that would haunt him at trial. He told Blackbird that he would testify that a "nigger" did it and had tried to blame Benny. The use of that particular pejorative had long since lost any social cachet that it once had in this country, particularly in Birmingham, Alabama. And Benny's casual use of it would come back to haunt him. Benny's remarks were memorialized on a detailed interview form which was mailed to the Jefferson County Sheriff's Department and then into the district attorney's case file. The Sioux warrior had found a way to stick it to another pale face in a moment months down the road that would rival Little Big Horn as a great event in Indian history.

Roger and I had checked Benny's criminal history and he had two prior felony convictions for burglary. Ordinarily, this record would be sufficient to keep a defendant from testifying since the fact of his convictions would be inadmissible at trial unless the defendant elected to testify. And even then, jurors would be instructed by the judge that they could use the fact of those convictions only to assess the defendant's credibility, not that he would be prone to commit the presently charged offense just because he had twice been convicted of other crimes.

But several days prior to trial Roger and I had discussed the possibility that Benny's large ego would impel him to testify. Further, that he might just be stupid enough to tell the same story that he had related to Louis Blackbird, only using a more socially acceptable term for the imaginary African-American that Benny had created in telling Blackbird what his defense at trial would be. Even Benny Martin was not so stupid as to use the *other* word in open court.

In anticipation of using Blackbird as a rebuttal witness in the event that Benny Martin would testify, we contacted the old reservation policeman and made arrangements to fly him to Birmingham without benefit of subpoena. By avoiding serving him with a subpoena, we also ensured that his name appeared nowhere in the court file. Thus, if the defendant's attorney happened to check the file on the day of trial —and he did – he would not know that we had a witness stashed away. Some of the old timers around the courthouse used to refer to this ploy as having a "bush" witness, meaning that you stashed him away until you had the opportunity to call him to the stand. Of course, by not using such a witness in your case-in-chief, you were running the risk of the defendant not testifying on his own behalf.

Roger and I had our Indian time bomb stashed at a downtown

motel very close to the courthouse. But we still were taking a chance that Benny might not testify, which, if such turned out to be the case, Blackbird couldn't testify either since we were saving him to rebut Benny's anticipated testimony. Our boss, David Barber, probably wouldn't appreciate the cost of the round trip plane ticket from North Dakota as well as the cost of a nice motel room for two nights. Something just told us that we'd damn well better find a way to use Blackbird as a witness or we might be joining him back on the reservation. And the chief also ran up a large telephone bill and some rather steep charges for room service and liquor that we didn't know about until he was back in the Friendly Skies.

Roger and I whistled past the graveyard as to what we'd do if we saved Blackbird as a possible rebuttal witness and then were not able to use him if Benny didn't testify. We jokingly agreed that if that scenario unfolded, in light of all the money we'd spent on Blackbird, we'd simply tell the boss that the Indian had testified, and that he was a great witness. In short, we'd lie and hope that David didn't notice the absence of our own star witness from our case.

Fortunately, since we had put all of our chips on the table betting that Benny couldn't help himself, he didn't disappoint us and took the stand. On direct examination, Benny had enough sense not to assert, as he had so indelicately termed it when in a jail cell with Louis Blackbird, that the main player was a "nigger." After all, he could still blame the murder on somebody else without offending the fine African American jurors who made up approximately half the jury. He simply said that the real killer was some black guy, evidently believing that it was still 1963 in Birmingham, and that his racist lie would be bought by the jury. But he didn't know that we had the Indian stashed in an office deep in the bowels of the courthouse, primed to clobber Benny with his own words from his stay in a Minnesota lockup.

I then witnessed a cross examination conducted by Roger Brown that resembled nothing so much as an anatomically correct dissection of a soon-to-be cadaver executed by a master surgeon. Roger skinned Benny alive before the thug even knew that he had been wounded. The first thing that Roger did was to lock down Benny into the tale he had spun for the jury on his direct examination, only with much more detail.

Benny obviously believed that he could outsmart Roger Brown, a trait that only underscored Benny's stupidity. He testified that on the night of the murder, before getting together with his younger friends who actually committed the murder, he had gone to a couple of stripper bars which he frequented on a regular basis. What an opening for Roger! He immediately followed up on Benny's boastful account of his going to the stripper bars with the question: "Well, I guess you're really a macho kind of guy?" Benny bit like the fool on the hill. "Yeah, I guess you could say that."

From that point forward in the trial, Roger Brown addressed Benny, or referred to him, not as Mr. Martin but as "Macho Man." Erskine Mathis, Benny's defense attorney, more or less had to let Roger get away with this stunt, because objecting to his client's being referred to as "Macho Man" only served to emphasize to the jury the circumstances which led to Benny's new moniker. After Roger finished his dissection of Benny, the ball game was all over but the cryin' and the shoutin'.

And when Roger asked him, "well, isn't it a fact that you told a cell mate, a Mr. Louis Blackbird, that you were going to say that a cnigger' did the killing?" With Roger's spitting out that word like a piece of rotten fruit, every member of that jury – black and white

– sat straight up and visibly bristled. Poor Benny could do nothing but meekly deny it, whereupon Roger questioned him in detail about what Benny had said to Blackbird. Roger even showed Benny the police report to "refresh" Benny's recollection. The report spelled out in detail what the old reservation policeman who was in jail for fighting told the local police on the very day that Benny mouthed those words that had now returned to haunt him. And the "Macho Man" could do nothing but stick to his now totally unbelievable story. It was sweet.

After Benny's rebirth as "Macho Man" and subsequent metaphorical castration performed by Roger Brown, the defense rested after being eviscerated by Roger's surgically perfect cross examination. We the State then summoned Louis Blackbird to testify before the jury. Benny, of course, recognized him immediately, and his alabaster skin flushed the brightest crimson you can imagine in front of that jury. I conducted the rebuttal questioning and thoroughly enjoyed it. In response to my questions, the reincarnation of Crazy Horse proceeded to gut Benny like a hog being dressed out to yield enough bacon to feed the congregation of the local First Baptist Church. It was a treat to watch the "Macho Man" have the macho knocked right out of him. And he didn't flinch when he looked the jury square in their eyes and told them exactly what Benny had told him including that very offensive word. Erskine Mathis did the best that he could but the old chief wouldn't budge.

I gave the first closing argument for the prosecution and merely hammered home the evidence in an orderly fashion for the jury. Mathis, a tall former police officer who looked like the Marlboro man – complete with mustache and cowboy boots – worked with what he could, mainly trying to discredit our witnesses and pin the murder on them. Funny, he never mentioned Lewis Blackbird or the jailhouse statement that Benny made to him.

Roger Brown then delivered one of the most powerful closing arguments that I have ever heard. He played the jury the way that Isaac Stern plays a Stradivarius, achieving a perfect synchronicity between his oratory and the emotions of the jury. The final note in the symphony was a brief story that Roger told about the family of the murdered young man sitting down at a family reunion a few years down the road, and a young boy asking his mother why there was an empty chair at the table. His mother responds by telling her young son that his daddy would have been sitting there but that his life had been taken by the "Macho Man." At least half the members of the jury were crying openly, and I even had to fight back the tears welling up in my eyes. It was everything that trial advocacy is supposed to be and rarely is except in the movies.

That jury convicted Benny Martin in an almost embarrassingly brief period of time and the judge sentenced him on the spot to a term of life in the penitentiary. Lesson to be learned: If you are a defendant and Roger Brown is the prosecutor, just run up the white flag and seek mercy. Erskine Mathis has never completely gotten over our bringing Lewis Blackbird from some reservation in North Dakota to drive the last nail into Benny Martin's coffin.

EVIL PERSONIFIED – ANTHONY RAY HINTON

THERE WERE SCORES OF other cases that I prosecuted, some memorable, others quickly and easily forgotten. These cases afforded me the opportunity to exact at least some semblance of justice as I had believed in that concept prior to becoming a prosecutor. And when I speak of justice, I tried to employ a sliding scale in meting out that sometimes amorphous entity which came as close as possible to my personal concept of justice and to avoid making arbitrary decisions as best I could. Put in simpler terms, I tried to draw distinctions between basically good people who had done something stupid, but illegal, and the rat bastards who should have been worked over with a Louisville Slugger and then drawn and quartered.

And speaking of rat bastards, one of the coldest executioners that I ever confronted in all my years as a prosecutor was Anthony Ray Hinton, a/k/a "the Cooler Killer." In late February of 1985, John Davidson, the night manager of the Mrs. Winner's fried chicken restaurant, located on Birmingham's Southside, a nice area of the city and home of numerous businesses as well as private dwellings, was found in the restaurant, barely alive, having been shot twice in the head. He was found after 2:00 a.m. by the pest control employee who had come by to spray the interior of the restaurant. There was a blood trail leading from the walk-in freezer to Davidson's body which was several feet outside the freezer. He had been shot twice in the head and died by the time he was transported to the hospital.

Since Davidson's wallet was found by the police in the parking lot next to his car, it appeared that he had closed out the cash register and locked up, and was in the process of walking to his car when he was accosted and directed back into the building. Inside the restaurant evidence technicians and detectives found the safe open with no money in it, the alarm disconnected and the door unlocked, indicating obviously that the killer left through the same door that he and Davidson had used to enter the building. The evidence techs also dusted all of the likely places for fingerprints – the safe, door, counter tops, etc. – but found no prints. The case was assigned to Detective Butch Quinn, an experienced and thorough investigator.

Quinn followed crime scene protocol and employed all standard investigative procedures just as he had been trained to do and had done on many prior occasions. Normally, any crime investigation of a business would include interviews of any and all potential witnesses, including a screen of the neighbors as well as a thorough examination of the crime scene and interviews of all employees, just for starters. Quinn followed all of these steps and turned up nothing. He also put the word out on the street, hoping that an informant or somebody looking for more favorable treatment on a pending case would point the finger at the perpetrator. Nothing.

And so it went for the next several months. People continued to kill each other, usually for some matter of real importance, such as "dissing" someone at a local club or killing the wife because she didn't have dinner ready when her husband decided he was hungry. I do not exaggerate. I prosecuted Frank Leo Walton for shooting and killing his wife because she put his hot meal on the kitchen counter instead of on the table directly in front of him. But it seemed that the Mrs. Winner's robbery-murder might just move into the realm of the unsolved crime drawer, unless the unexpected occurred and history repeated itself. The cold of winter passed, the beauty and freshness of spring came and went, and finally the searing oven of the summer months descended on Birmingham, and still not a hint as to who had robbed Mrs. Winners and killed John Davidson in late February.

That situation changed dramatically on the night of July first / second at another fast food restaurant, this being a Captain D's in a well populated business locale in the Eastern area of the city. I arrived at work early that morning and the District Attorney, David Barber, told me that there had been a robbery and a murder and that I should accompany him to the scene. I readily complied and we went in David's car to the Captain D's in Woodlawn. Prior to the start of the business day on the second of July, the regional manager of the restaurant, Ruben Valdez, went to the restaurant to pick up the previous day's cash. The door to the restaurant was unlocked, the safe was open and Wayne Vason, the shift manager from the night before, was lying dead in the cooler, two bullet holes in his head. Just as at the Mrs. Winner's robbery in February, there were no finger-prints or clues of any other kind.

Since the murder of John Davidson at Mrs. Winner's had oc-curred several months before this particular robbery-murder, no one at the scene had made the connection by the time that the boss and I arrived. The investigator from the robbery and homicide division of the Birmingham Police Department who happened to be "in the barrel" when the call came in to the division was Detective Sergeant Howard Miller. He was very experienced in working homicides and had great instincts as well.

Like most good cops, Miller could go to a crime scene, and merely through experience and observation tell you pretty well what happened and how it happened, and also tell you the type of per-petrator if the identity was unknown. The FBI has a unit of agents who study crime scenes, psychology of criminals and several other disciplines to do the same things that a good street cop does without the label of "behavioral scientist" and the imprimatur of the Bureau. And Howard Miller was a good street cop. He knew what to look for, how to interpret what he found and how to interrogate suspects. He also had an abundance of common sense which was invaluable in narrowing the scope of his investigations.

When David Barber and I arrived on the scene, the parking lot was already cordoned off and the uniforms and evidence techs were tending to their responsibilities. Miller was talking to a couple of the uniforms, making sure that assignments were communicated and completed. Barber and Miller then began talking about the crime, and Miller demonstrated to David the locking mechanism on the side door leading to the kitchen, as well as the fact that it was in the unlocked position when Valdez had arrived earlier that morning. After a brief period of time, Miller recognized the similarity between this crime scene and the Mrs. Winner's crime scene the previous February. He directed one of his subordinates to notify the morgue and the Department of Forensic Sciences to run a comparison ASAP between the bullets removed from John Davidson and those to be removed from Wayne Vason.

By mid-afternoon the comparison had been made and the bullets matched. The meaning of those results was obvious; there was one robber and he was eliminating witnesses. Sgt. Miller and I worked the entire day. Miller made sure that potential witnesses were interviewed and that other directives were carried out, while I was just being with him trying to soak up everything I could from the veteran homicide detective.

One interesting development was brought to our attention late in the afternoon. We learned that several young black males had been arrested earlier that day and charged with the burglary of a business the night before, and that one of them had a .38 caliber revolver that had been fired twice recently. John Davidson and Wayne Vason each had been shot twice with a pistol of the same caliber. Additionally, these young men all had coin wrappers of the same type used to wrap coins at Captain D's. And the business that they burglarized was a scant eight blocks from Captain D's.

Those facts were enough to convince me that these young thugs likely were our killers. I expressed that thought to Miller and he said that it was possible but highly unlikely. Being certain of my seat of the pants opinion, I immediately challenged Miller's conclusion and asserted that surely these characters were the "doers". With a patience borne only from years of suffering fools, Detective Sergeant Howard Miller quietly explained to me that the guy who did these crimes was one person, probably in his early thirties, likely black and a convicted felon who had served time and had robbed people before the two robbery murders that we now knew he committed. Also, that the gun that he was using likely belonged to his mama or an auntie.

I still was not convinced and so I said something intelligent along the lines of: "Okay, Sherlock, tell me how it is that you arrived at your conclusions – mental telepathy, or are you just blowing smoke up my boxer shorts?" Miller just smiled, and then took the time to explain his conclusions to me. And I learned what being an intuitive investigator, whose intuitions had been sharpened from years of experience, was all about. What he next told me made such absolute sense that I could have kicked myself for not coming to the same conclusions independent of Miller.

"This guy is probably in his early thirties because after the Mrs. Winner's job, Butch Quinn never got a whisper from the street. A kid would have run his mouth to his buddies. He has done time, probably for robbery. He's black and the pistol that he used was not his, because he's careful not to use it except when doing a robbery. He likely was looking at a very long stretch in prison if he's caught with it. And he's probably black because of where Mrs. Winner's and Captain D's are located; it's just playing the odds. A white thug likely would be hitting places out in the county. Forensics said that the pistol was worn almost smooth inside the barrel, indicating that it was old, probably a family pistol that our guy would use when doing a job."

Later in the summer, after the "Cooler Killer" had been arrested, his profile made Miller look like a prophet. Anthony Ray Hinton was a twenty-nine year old black male who lived with his mother, the owner of a very old pistol with the inner barrel worn down to a significant extent because it had been fired many times. Hinton had three felony convictions for either theft or burglary and one robbery in the first degree arrest which had been dismissed at a preliminary hearing because the female victim couldn't identify Hinton in open court sufficiently accurately enough to please the judge.

And just as in the murder of John Davidson, night manager of Mrs. Winner's, the bad guy accosted Wayne Vason outside in the parking lot after he had locked up for the night, forced him at gunpoint to unlock the back door, cleaned out the safe after disconnecting the alarm, made Vason get in the cooler and then shot him twice in the head. And just like Mrs. Winner's he left no finger prints. Howard Miller would earn his pay on this case. And that opportunity would come sooner than any of us anticipated.

On the night of July 25, 1985, the night manager of Quincy's Restaurant in the Bessemer Division of Jefferson County became the luckiest man in Alabama, not too long after almost becoming just another piece of decaying flesh on a cold slab at the county morgue destined for his final place of rest on Boot Hill. Sid Smotherman, a fifty-five year old man who had worked at Quincy's for several years, was aware of the first two murders because Detective Sergeant Howard Miller had spread the word among fast-food managers throughout the county. Smotherman was one of those managers and he took the warning seriously enough to make certain that all of his employees knew the *modus operandi* of the killer, and that they all should be particularly careful and alert at closing time. Indeed, that any employees who left at closing time should leave in a group.

Including Smotherman, there were three or four workers on the last shift of the day, all of whom left the business together at closing time. Mr. Smotherman left and then drove in his car alone and went to a supermarket located several blocks from Quincy's. One other employee went by separate car to the same market. While inside, he noticed a "strange" looking man watching Mr. Smotherman, but thought nothing more about it at the time. This sighting was important in the later identification of the shooter.

After purchasing a six pack of beer, Smotherman left the store, got in his car and was driving home when his car was bumped by another car directly behind his on the otherwise deserted street. Sid then made the mistake that nearly cost him his life; he stopped his car and went to address the situation with the other driver. A woman in a similar situation would stop her car – if she stopped at all – only at a lighted service station or upon seeing a police officer. We men are brought up with the notion of handling our own problems, particularly one as seemingly innocuous as a little fender bender, even one that occurs at night when no one else except the driver of the other car is present. Just more proof that women are smarter than men.

Smotherman was hurriedly ushered at gunpoint into the car driven by the bad guy and directed to drive back quickly to Quincy's. During the drive the big man with the big gun kept urging Smotherman to drive faster because he had to drive to Atlanta that night to meet another person. Of course the real reason had nothing to do with driving to Atlanta but everything to do with solidifying his alibi. When they arrived back at the restaurant, Smotherman obeyed the command to unlock the door and open the safe. Those tasks having been completed, the man with the gun ordered Smotherman to get in the freezer. If he had not figured it out on the drive back to Quincy's, Sid surely knew when he heard those words that he had but seconds to live. And it was that knowledge which gave him the gumption to do what he next did, and which saved his life.

Sid Smotherman had his wits about him and he used them under the kind of pressure that I can only vaguely imagine. He told his would-be executioner that it was "cold in the freezer, that he knew he would have to stay in there all night, and could he go into the vegetable locker instead of the freezer?" The man with the gun could have shot him where he stood, but the shots might be heard outside the store. And it was vitally important to him that the sound of gunfire not be heard by any casual passer by.

What he didn't know, and what Smotherman was hopeful that he would not figure out, was that the food locker door was already opened a crack, but that upon being pushed open enough for someone to enter, it was also locked from the inside and would simply have to be slammed shut for the lock to engage. And that knowledge, quick thinking and fast acting is what saved Sid's life.

As he pushed open the door, he turned to face the angel of death. As he was turning he saw that the "Cooler Killer" had the pistol leveled at his head. Sid screamed as his would-be executioner fired the pistol twice while he held it with both hands. Simultaneously with his screams and the explosions caused by the shots, Sid ducked and felt the pain caused by one bullet striking him on the forehead and the other hitting his finger, because his natural reaction was to try to block the bullet any way he could. But he did manage to slam the door shut from inside the food locker which engaged the lock and created a barrier between him and the gun.

After about ten minutes, the pain was so bad that Sid took a chance and unlocked the door. He then managed to get outside the store and wave down a car being driven by a Birmingham Stallions professional football player whose date was accompanying him. She happened to be a nurse, and the couple picked up Smotherman and rushed him to the hospital.

Fortunately, he wasn't hurt badly, just painfully and with the bejeebers scared right out of him. His index finger had the tip blown away and he had a vertical path under his facial skin where the bullet had failed to go directly into his skull. It actually exited from his neck, below his chin and was found in his shirt pocket. For real! And the bullet that hit his finger tip was found on a shelf back in the food locker. The end path of the two bullet projectiles obviously indicated that they were very low velocity firings, probably from a very old gun. And aside from Sid surviving the ordeal, the best news – except for the "Cooler Killer" – was that the recovered bullets matched those from the Mrs. Winner's and Captain D's victims.

The good luck just kept happening to the investigation. The Bessemer Police Department had the good sense to use the services of a local artist who worked for the Bessemer Star newspaper who, after working closely with Smotherman, produced a picture of the man who tried to kill him. The result was a very detailed sketch of the man which Smotherman affirmed looked just like the man who had shot him. It was much more detailed than one of those look-like just-about-anybody products of an Identikit layover with several sheets of plastic, each having a different facial component, with the end result looking only coincidentally human.

This sketch looked like an identifiable human being and the good fortune kept happening when it was shown to each of the employees. A young man named Reginald White not only recognized the sketch as being a dead ringer for Anthony Ray Hinton, he had seen Hinton not two weeks prior to the robbery and attempted murder and had a conversation with him. White told investigators that Hinton questioned him closely about the night manager and the type car that he drove, as well as other questions concerning the Quincy's where White worked. At the time, while such questioning seemed somewhat unusual to White, he just marked it off as Hinton being as strange as he always had been. But Hinton was already planning his next robbery/murder and he was actually gathering information from the unwitting White.

The police knew all about Hinton from prior adverse dealings with him. Following White's supplying them with Hinton's name after inspecting the sketch, and following Sid Smotherman's positive identification of the man depicted in the sketch as the man who robbed and tried to kill him, members of the Bessemer Police Department and deputies from the Jefferson County Sheriff's Department went immediately to his mother's house where Anthony Ray had a bedroom of his own. There was Hinton in the front yard cleaning his car, not the one described by Smotherman. The Bessemer police asked Hinton if he minded whether they searched his car and he told them to go right ahead. They found nothing and went ahead and arrested him. And if it hadn't been for a grizzled old deputy named Clyde Amberson who was there from the sheriff's department, all of their evidence would essentially be Sid Smotherman's identification which any defense attorney worth his ability to mislead a jury could break.

Amberson knew that Hinton's mother owned a pistol, and she confirmed his belief when he asked her about it. However, it wasn't where she normally left it in the kitchen and she began looking for it throughout the house. It turned up hidden under the mattress in her bedroom, and it was an old gun, the interior of the barrel having been worn down over the years, just as Lauden Yates had said it would be weeks prior to Hinton being identified as the man who robbed and attempted to murder Smotherman. She turned it over to

Amberson. Upon test firing and comparing the spent projectiles to those from the three crime scenes, it was a match. Had it not been for Amberson's quick thinking, Anthony Ray Hinton could be walking the streets today.

This sociopath with a glare as steady and cold as the polar ice cap in winter went before a jury of his peers in September of 1986. The trial was held in the old Jefferson County Courthouse, the last criminal case tried in that building. The new Criminal Justice Center has since been used strictly for the trial of criminal cases. Steve Mahon was my trial partner in the Hinton case and he did a superb job of cross-examining Hinton's "expert" on the matter of the bullet comparisons.

We were fortunate in that two forensics tool marks comparison experts who worked for the Alabama Department of Forensic Sciences each independently matched up the spent projectiles from the two murders and the one attempted murder as having been fired from the same firearm. And when the suspected weapon was recovered from Hinton's mother's house, they matched up the recovered projectiles from it. David Higgins was a solid and experienced forensic scientist and Lauden Yates was one of the most experienced and foremost experts in the country. Hinton still awaits his fate on Alabama's death row, having virtually exhausted all of his state and federal avenues of appeal, but for one, which now reposes on the docket of the Alabama Supreme Court awaiting their ruling on an issue which all of us involved in the case thought had been resolved at trial.

Hinton, some ten years after his conviction, and through his *pro bono* attorneys, who never found a guilty man on death row, raised the issue that his trial attorney, Sheldon Perhacs, was incompetent for calling as an expert witness a man who was eviscerated on cross examination by Steve Mahon. (Funny, I thought that's what lawyers were supposed to do to adverse witnesses.) And so, the projectiles sat around for ten years, subject to the effects of oxidation, and two hired guns came into court and testified that they couldn't determine whether the projectiles were fired by the weapon seized from Hinton's momma's house, but that at least two of the projectiles, *in their expert opinion*, were not fired from the same gun.

And of course, Hinton has become the new flavor of the week by the anti-death-penalty gangsters, excuse me, *zealots*. I have nothing but respect for any individual who is opposed to the death penalty for religious or moral reasons, or for that matter, no reason at all, but for pity's sake, please quit trying to make heroes out of these thugs and don't assert across the board that they're all innocent. In other words, just be intellectually honest. As an aside, Sheldon Perhacs just happens to be, and was at the time that he represented Hinton, one of the most respected and *way beyond competent* criminal defense attorneys in the state.

My co-counsel, Steve Mahon, also located a person who broke Hinton's alibi for the night of the Quincy's job. That alibi consisted of Hinton's time card from the warehouses where he worked, as well as supporting testimony from one of the managers of the business that owned the warehouses to the effect that there was only one entrance and one exit through the fence which encircled the warehouses. Further, that both the entrance and the exit joined into one passageway through the shack in which the time clock was located, and that there was always a guard in the shack to ensure that nobody punch more than one time card.

Thus, Hinton had a relatively brief window of time in which to leave, drive to Quincy's, snatch Smotherman, and finally to make Smotherman open the safe and then go into the cooler where Hinton could murder him. And that's why Hinton kept commanding the older gentleman to drive faster after he got the drop on him. Important to note is that Hinton worked in the warehouse *by himself*, and that his supervisor walked around the warehouse, occasionally seeing Hinton while making his rounds.

Of course, we destroyed that alibi by locating the night security guard who was working the gate that night and who had since joined the army and was stationed at a post somewhere in the mid west, and flying him back for trial. He was a great witness who testified that those time cards didn't always actively reflect accurately how long a given employee was at work on any particular night. He also testified that it was not uncommon on any given night for more than one or two employees to leave for a short period of time, usually to retrieve something from their car, and not punch out on the time clock. Finally, he testified that there were one or two holes in the fence big enough to allow anyone to enter or leave without going through the entrance/exit and totally avoid the time clock.

The trial itself was unique in that it was the first, and I believe still only, Alabama trial in which two totally separate capital murders were joined for one trial. Additionally, every single piece of evidence in the Quincy's case had to be introduced in the two cases before the jury, even though Quincy's was in a different jurisdiction and technically, the robbery and attempted murder of Mr. Smotherman could not be tried in the Birmingham Division of Jefferson County.

This jurisdictional anomaly had to be overcome by overriding the legal principle that normally prohibited the introduction of evidence of one or more separate bad acts to help prove another. Exceptions are granted at the discretion of the trial judge when identity of the offender is at issue. When proof of one or more uncharged crimes is necessary to prove the identity of the offender in the charged offense, introduction of evidence of the uncharged crimes may be admitted by the judge.

Simply speaking, evidence of all the crimes charged, if sufficiently similar, should be allowed in order to prove the identity of the offender. In the two capital cases being tried, the bullets from all three offenses were a match. And they were linked by Sid Smotherman's identification as the man who shot him. Additionally, the *modus operandi* was virtually identical in all three cases. The law recognizes that, when identity of the offender is at issue, there exists a necessity to allow the jury to see and/or hear evidence of uncharged offenses. Obviously, the details of all three incidents were more than sufficiently similar to allow their admission into evidence. That, plus the testimony of the State's firearms and tool-mark experts that the same firearm was used in each of the three incidents, and that the bullet projectiles recovered in all three instances were fired from the same gun recovered from Hinton's house, was the crux of the State's case.

The trial itself was filled with drama, but the result strangely enough, was almost a foregone conclusion. Not that our case was some sort of evidentiary crusher, although it was solid and we felt impervious to any real challenge from the defense. It simply was well put together and had the right "fit" to it. But more so than the evidence, I have never had as strong a feeling in trying any other case that the defendant just radiated guilt and pure evil as much as in the Hinton trial. I gave probably as strong an opening statement as I ever have, before or since, and when I sat down at counsel table after my opening, I was totally relaxed and knew intuitively that the jury would convict.

During the trial there were at least two moments of prime drama, the first when Sid Smotherman testified, the second when Hinton himself surprisingly took the stand. I know that I have never witnessed a statement as fraught with drama as when Smotherman responded to my question about what he did when Hinton pointed the old pistol at him and told him to get into the freezer: "I just said to myself, 'Goodbye, Babe,' and I stepped toward the freezer." Now *that* is high drama.

Number two was more shocking but it underscored for the jury just how cold Hinton was. I had him on cross examination and he had denied using his momma's pistol to commit his crimes. After I established that only he and his mother had access to the gun, I asked him with more than a touch of sarcasm in my voice whether it was his contention that his mother had been the gunman. Instead of continuing to deny that the gun in the house was not the one used in the crimes, his response was chilling: "Well, she could have been." That answer rocked the courtroom.

Just the way in which Hinton gave his ill-considered response erased any possible lingering doubt as to his guilt. The jury was out for only an hour of deliberations as they convicted Hinton of capital murder in both the Mrs. Winner's case as well as the Captain D's case. Unfortunately, twenty-three years after the trial, Hinton sits on death row as his various appeals and writs wend their way through the maze of both state and federal appeals courts before justice finally can be served.

An interesting sidelight to this drama is the relationship that I developed with Hinton during all of the pre-trial hearings, as well as the trial itself. At his arraignment, Mahon handled the serving of the indictment while I just looked at Hinton. Unlike most defendants who will merely glance at the prosecutor, ARH just stared right back at me. I made it a point not to blink; Hinton also held steady. To have weakened would have been tantamount to lowering the colors and running up the white flag of surrender.

By unspoken agreement, we continued our face-off throughout every pre-trial proceeding, with Steve Mahon handling legal proceedings for the State and Sheldon Perhacs making defense arguments. All the while, Hinton and I would expend our collective energy trying to laser a hole, each through the other. It got to the point where it was almost pathological, with each of us refusing to break off. Over the course of the year between arrest and trial, our unspoken relationship became very personal. Hinton epitomized the essence of evil as far as I was concerned, and I felt certain that he would like nothing better than to add me to his list of victims. And by the fashion and dogged determination with which he returned my glare, it was obvious that our showdown was straight from whatever deep inside us made us that way.

As I said, it took the jury only an hour, most of which likely was spent drinking coffee and electing a foreman, to pronounce their verdict. The sentencing phase also took only about an hour. In Alabama in a capital case, the sentence returned by the jury is advisory only. The judge has the authority either to accept or reject the jury's recommendation. In this case, no one doubted what he would do. Judge Garret imposed the actual sentence at a formal hearing several weeks after the trial.

At that time, Hinton testified extemporaneously and non-stop for forty-five minutes. I will never forget his opening sentence spoken directly to me: "Mr. McGregor, when this (prosecution) started, I hated you and your hateful eyes. But now I love you, and when the real killer is found, I will be there to tell you how much that I love you." I remember thinking at the time that I would meet him at the prison gates if he were ever to be released, and that it wouldn't be with either love in my heart or air in my hands. He addressed me by name twice more during his oration, and nothing changed in his demeanor or in the evil he projected. Judge Garret then sentenced him to die in the electric chair. And almost a quarter of a century later, he remains on death row while the relatives of his two victims suffer silently as a growing legion of do-gooders and other useful idiots proclaim Hinton's innocence to anyone who will listen.

Chapter Seven

A CHANGE OF PACE – A LITTLE COP,
CONVICT AND COURTROOM HUMOR

AMIDST ALL OF THIS high drama and stomach churning angst of murders, rapes and other atrocities that humans inflict on each other however, are flashes of graveyard humor, a common commodity in the business of crime and punishment. Much of what passes for humor among cops, prosecutors, defense attorneys, and the other assorted courthouse rats is not at all humorous, but tragic to normal citizens. But some of it is genuinely funny, "and I don't care who you are," as Larry the Cable Guy would say. And some is merely bizarre. You be the judge.

The first tale of macabre humor overcoming the natural sadness attendant to human misery is one in which I was not present. In fact, it preceded my career as a prosecutor, but it lives on in the telling and retelling that has it enshrined in the trove of cop stories that survive even after the principals have retired or otherwise left the fraternity of the badge. Some twenty-five or so years ago when David Barber was a deputy district attorney, as well as a gun-toting, fist-fighting, first prosecutor at the scene of the crime, any crime, and also a friend of any good cop, he and a few of his buddies in blue were knocking back some cool ones at the end of a particularly hot summer's day in the city. I'm not certain but I believe that the crime fighters included Paul Price, of Birmingham Homicide Division and possibly Jay Glass, Deputy Coroner of Jefferson County.

As the sun was about to set over the yardarm, pagers started going off and calls were made in response. It seemed that someone in a neighborhood not too far from the watering hole where the aforementioned had stationed themselves, a citizen reported detecting a strange aroma wafting on the breeze and seeming to emanate from a particular domicile which apparently had been *sans* its sole occupant for about the past week to ten days. When the cavalry arrived after a hasty departure from the local watering hole and social club, they made entry into the house and were almost overcome with the putrid stench of decomposing flesh.

After a quick survey of the main room and the kitchen, the band of brothers entered the bedroom where the aroma grew even stronger. The intrepid gum shoes then reluctantly shoved open the bathroom door. That feat required some degree of effort from one of the advance team, since the wooden barrier had been secured by towels jammed between it and the floor. Inside the bathroom was a window that had been taped close. There was also a small charcoal burner that contained nothing but dead coals and ashes.

But these accouterments were not what hit the detectives squarely in the eye (not to mention the nose) upon making entry. Almost in the exact middle of the small room was the royal throne. But *this* throne had a king perched on it. A very dead king. The sight of a naked man who must have weighed two hundred fifty pounds *ante mortem* was so disgusting it was obscene. Saying that the body was "ripe" is a gross understatement. Remember, this was Birmingham in the summer and it was like living in a kettle of hot soup. It took about tem minutes for the good guys to do a preliminary screening and processing of the scene and then to notify the coroner's office to summon the meat wagon to the house.

After a brief discussion all parties agreed that the poor soul had committed suicide in the most bizarre manner that any of them had ever seen or heard about in all of their collective years in law enforcement. The small charcoal burner was used to consume all of the oxygen in the little bathroom which had been hermetically sealed with towels and tape. The result was death by self-inflicted suffocation.

The atmosphere initially had been somewhat somber, but the realization that what they saw in the bathroom was the product of suicide and not murder induced a more relaxed atmosphere. One of the group began joking that charcoal burners should be banned because it was obvious that they were inherently dangerous. And without skipping a beat, one of the detectives got deadly serious and stated for posterity's sake a bastardization of a then popular bumper sticker: *"When hibachis are outlawed, only outlaws will have hibachis."* When the laughter stopped, the intrepid heroes quickly finished their business and headed back to the social club.

Perhaps the funniest one liner that I ever heard uttered in a court of law came from the lips of one of two defendants being tried for capital murder. Donnis Musgrove and David Rogers were being tried together, upon their motion and over my objection, for the capital murder of one Coy "Mooter" Barron. He had been a proud home renter in the less than plush Robinwood section of the Magic City, also known as "the white man's North Birmingham." "Mooter" lived in the one-bedroom rental house with his nineteen-year-old-wife Libby, and their infant daughter, Amber. My memory is that he worked for a small timber clearing business, and possibly sold a little weed on the side. And that enterprise is likely what got him killed.

Mooter met his maker in September of 1986 at about 2:00 one

morning in his own bedroom wearing nothing but fear on his face and black knee stockings on his legs. He and Libby and baby Amber were in the bedroom trying to sleep. It was a restless sleep. Mooter kept getting up and looking out the window. Earlier that night a man named Tony Morgan came by the house and Mooter went outside and spoke with him. After talking with Tony, Mooter was visibly nervous and tossed and turned next to Libby. Tony, you see, was both a friend of Mooter, as well as the son of Larry Morgan, reputed to be a seller of *primo* weed and also a very tough guy. And therein lays the possible motive for the break-in and murder.

The word around the neighborhood was that Mooter had stolen about forty pounds of marijuana from Larry Morgan, and that Morgan wanted his money and the thief who stole it. That thief may have been Coy "Mooter" Barron, or may have been someone else, but Larry Morgan believed it was Mooter. And Larry Morgan used other thugs to do his heavy work. One of those thugs was Donnis Musgrove. And in the late night hours of that date in September, Coy Barron's last on earth, Musgrove and David Rogers broke into his house and shot him dead in front of his wife and baby. This act of ultimate violence was somewhat out of character since both were professional car thieves by trade. But no one doubted that they were capable of murder if the price was right.

About two months later, they were captured in a multi-county high speed chase. Neither has tasted freedom since that day. Rogers, in fact, died several years ago while on Death Row, thus effectively cheating the hangman. Musgrove continues to languish in his small cage while his seemingly endless appeals and writs continue to wend their way through both the State as well as the Federal legal labyrinth. But that's putting the car before the theft if you'll pardon my lame attempt at humor. First, a little history of our two villains,

Donnis George Musgrove and his partner in murder, the now deceased David Walter Rogers. And I can't neglect the man who made this case with some of the best and most dogged investigative work that I enjoyed as a prosecutor in the District Attorney's Office, my close personal friend, Howard "Ho, Ho" Brooks. We became brothers during the course of this investigation and subsequent trial.

Musgrove and Rogers might just as well have been brothers. And, in a very real sense they were brothers – brothers in crime, that is. Each of them had twenty-six (you read that correctly) prior felony convictions. And each of them had escaped that summer from work release. Musgrove had simply walked off the job in June and Rogers escaped in July from the van that was transporting him to his work site. That last fact is most important because it illustrates the abysmal penal system in Alabama that permitted individuals with twenty-six prior felony convictions to enjoy the privileges of work release, and also because it gave Musgrove the opportunity to crack wise in an apparent attempt to break my concentration.

The case took about a year to come to trial. As I had earlier mentioned, the two defendants were jointly tried on their own motion and over my objection even though each was entitled to his own separate trial. The reason that they wanted to be tried together is because they had an alibi witness out of Florida and they thought that the alibi would work only one time. As it turned out, it didn't even work once. The jury convicted both of them for the crime of capital murder.

In Alabama there is a bifurcated system when capital murder is charged in an indictment. If there is a capital conviction in the guilt phase, the same jury considers aggravating and mitigating factors in the punishment phase. If the aggravating factors outweigh the mitigating factors, the jury is entitled to recommend the death penalty to the judge. The judge is entitled to accept or reject the jury's recommendation.

In this trial, after the jury found the defendants guilty, and as I was "putting on my game face" while I was walking from counsel table to stand before the jury, Donnis Musgrove got off his really funny line, worthy of anything that Henny Youngman used in one of his stand-up routines when Vaudeville was king. Judge Garrett heard him and had to turn his back to the jury in an effort to hide the grin on his face. I heard him and, in order to avoid laughing out loud, bit my lip so hard it almost bled.

Giving it his best shot while teetering on the brink of the precipice, Donnis put a little smile on his face and softly said: "*I guess this means that work release is out of the question, eh, Bob ?*" Grace under pressure is always uplifting to the observer. Donnis displayed it, but the jury wasn't buying what he was selling on this particular day. And to this day, his body and his spirit wither on death row until his personal Armageddon arrives and he meets his Maker.

Chapter Eight

THE BROKEN SOULS – TWO WHO SURVIVED
ALISA

I HAVE ALREADY WRITTEN to some extent about those less-than-human creatures that prey on children. But I have barely mentioned their victims, mainly because the nature of my business required me to find, destroy and prosecute the soul killers who assaulted these young angels. I had little opportunity to provide comfort and solace to these youngsters before moving on to the next prosecution. Most of the villains and more than a few of their victims remain etched in my memory. But at least two of the children – now adults – retain a very special place in my heart. And their tormentors, if God is just, will burn in hell for the rest of eternity when the dirt is thrown upon their dead, rotting bodies.

Alisa was her name and she was only eleven years old when the truth emerged, but she had suffered more in those years than most people endure in a lifetime. Had it not been for her brother's curiosity to find out why his sister was so secretive as to her journal entries, she might have taken her own life as she wrote in her diary, rather than to endure the horror of being raped on a consistent basis by her own father.

He was a fireman, respected by his peers as well as by his employer, the City of Hoover. His men in the department had confidence in his knowledge of firefighting and his coolness on the job. He had been married, had a son and a daughter, but couldn't get along with their mother, his former wife. But lots of men in his profession find it difficult to get along with their wives, and it didn't affect his ability to do his job.

And so he married a second time, this time to a woman who enjoyed a good time as much as anyone, and better than most. And they had no children to detract from their good times. But he still had visitation rights with his children, although their mother knew that Alisa would grow morose every time that she had to visit her father. And the little girl was too ashamed, embarrassed and hurt to let anyone know why she dreaded those visitations.

In one of those rare moments of serendipity, Alisa's brother – as brothers are wont to do – made a stealth raid on her diary and began reading. What he found in those pages horrified him. He went to her and revealed what he had done and what he had read. Her reaction was almost as frightening as her written words. She begged him to not tell her mother because of her shame and fear. And she told him that if he did so, she would commit suicide just as she had intimated in her diary. She exacted from him a promise that he would tell no one what had been happening to her for years at the hands of her father.

And the young boy intended to keep that promise but for the fact that he loved his sister too much to not do whatever he could do to rescue her from their own father. He went to his mother and asked her what he should do in a situation where someone was in trouble and needed help, but that he had promised to tell no one. Brenda, the mother of both the children, wisely counseled her son to share with her the secret that he held. She told him that if somebody really were to be in trouble that he would not break his promise by telling a person who could help. When her young son told her about the diary, its contents and what Alisa revealed to him, Brenda's blood ran cold.

Brenda had enough control of herself to understand that she had to contact the Hoover Police and let them conduct and guide the investigation. Such action was a dicey proposition because of the close relationship between the police department and the fire department. Fortunately, two sharp and experienced investigators, David Carlington and Laura Holt, drew the assignment. These two treated this investigation as they would any other – dispassionately, with no pre-conceived notions as to what and where it would take them.

They decided that the best way to test Alisa's allegation would be to have Brenda make a recorded call to her former husband in order to see whether he would make any damaging admissions. She made the call and told John that Alisa had come to her and told her everything that had been happening for years. John was caught completely off guard, and before he could gather his wits, he made some very incriminating statements that corroborated the allegations. The entire conversation was captured on tape.

And so it was that John Roper was charged with the forcible rape of his own daughter, Alisa, a rape that began occurring when she wasn't even old enough to know what was happening to her, only that her own daddy was hurting her and that she was shamed by him each time that it happened. By the time that her secret was exposed to her mother and to the police, Alisa was a fragile shell of a human being. She was suicidal and her psychiatrist warned that having to endure a trial might send her over the edge. Roper deserved to be in prison for the rest of his life, but I was faced with the possibility, actually the probability that even if Alisa didn't commit suicide, having to testify with her father sitting in court staring her down would damage her psychologically even more than she already had been traumatized.

Roper apparently thought that he could still beat the rap, and he had the gall to publicly proclaim his innocence despite his knowledge that he was on tape admitting his guilt. He even allowed his fellow firemen to paint his former wife Brenda as a trouble-making witch who had made up the story just because of her "hatred" of their friend John. They were good men, but they were terribly wrong about Brenda and their colleague and friend John. He was elevated to hero status by his fellow firefighters, and Brenda became the object of their own derision and misplaced loyalty.

Worse yet, the defense attorney knew that Alisa couldn't testify and that he might yet succeed in avoiding having to plead his client to serious, or any, prison time. Roper appeared to be a classic sexually abusive father, and not a pure pedophile who would necessarily pose a danger to any pre-pubescent child. In other words, he probably wasn't a real danger to any child at large. But what he had done to his own daughter for years was deserving of the worst punishment that society could impose on him. But he and his lawyer knew that Alisa likely couldn't withstand the rigors of a trial. That knowledge gave them a decided advantage in negotiating a guilty plea.

I could have amended the indictment and allowed Roper to enter a plea of guilty to the crime of incest, and there would have been no resulting conflagration of emotions and criticism from certain members of the press, including television and radio stations. The actual plea to the charge of Rape in the first degree ignited a firestorm throughout the community. Of course, in order to avoid the very publicity which would be so damaging to Alisa, none of the details of the offense could be made public.

The old maxim that no good deed goes unpunished seems to be an immutable law of nature. And this attempt at trying to both punish a child rapist as well as literally saving the life of the child, proved to be one of those instances. After consulting at length with both Brenda as well as with Detectives Carlington and Holt, I entered a plea agreement on behalf of the State with Roper and his lawyer.

The terms of the agreement were as follows: Roper would plead guilty to Rape in the first degree and be sentenced to a term of 15 years in the penitentiary. He would apply for, and the State would join him, in recommending probation. Should he receive probation, he would make a public apology to Brenda before each shift of the fire department for slandering her to his colleagues. Finally, he would pay for a video to be made and used as an educational tool in the community to educate the public about the dynamics of child sexual abuse. Such a video would feature an interview with him conducted by me and neither his nor Alisa's real names would be used.

The downside of the agreement was that, barring a violation of its terms, Roper would not go to prison. The upside was that Alisa would not have to be exposed to a trial that might drive her to take her own life. Had I amended the indictment and let Roper plead to incest, the world would never have noticed or cared. But there were two compelling reasons to not amend the indictment. First and foremost was the continued protection of Alisa and her identity. Should Roper plead to the crime of incest, the leap to identifying Alisa would be a mere hop and a skip. Or just a very short hop. And then all of her friends and schoolmates would know her awful secret. And Alisa would rather die than have to live with this knowledge being made known to the world. I refused to victimize her a second time. The second reason that I would not amend the indictment and receive a guilty plea to the crime of incest was that I wanted John Roper branded a rapist. He certainly was a rapist of the worst sort and, particularly since he likely would receive no prison time, he should be forced to wear that scarlet letter "R" for the rest of his sorry life.

But the nightmare was to follow. Newspapers, television and radio blasted me and the District Attorney for allowing a "rapist" to plead guilty to a probationary sentence with no more punishment than to apologize and to star in some video. At least that's how it was initially reported. Needless to say, the waste products hit the fan. The newspapers and all the other communications media smelled blood in the water. Fortunately, I had a hard earned reputation as both a very tough prosecutor as well as a stand-up guy for all victims, particularly for child abuse victims. With one notable exception, every reporter who covered the story asked me for an explanation after the initial explosion. And each of them honored my request to not print or otherwise communicate anything which might identify Alisa or her rapist father. All, save one radio commentator, were respectful of my position and my rationale for recommending probation for somebody whose crime certainly merited a life sentence.

The reaction from the public was fairly muted, particularly after the local chapter of VOCAL (Victims of Crime and Leniency), not to be confused with another organization employing the same acronym, Victims of Child Abuse Laws, made a public stand backing me and my decision. As I mentioned previously, however, there was one member of the broadcast media who, in an apparent effort to improve his dismal ratings, came after me hammer and tong, even after he was told the rationale for the plea and recommended sentence. This hack, Bob Gambacurta by name, faded from the scene some years ago, but not before I went to pay him a visit at his place of employment. I was just a bit hot under the collar, and the fighting Irish in me was in full blossom.

God must have intervened or I would likely have gotten myself fired and possibly jailed had he been at the station. But luck or the Almighty shined a protective light on me and the weasel Gambacurta was AWOL. His partner, a gentleman named Tim Lennox was the only person present, and he let me blow off the steam that had been building ever since his hack colleague had adopted the posture of the lone guardian of whatever Gambacurta deemed to be the appropriate measure of justice. He also was trying to make himself appear to be both the arbiter as well as the guardian of that public morality. It was obvious to him at least that the District Attorney's Office had abdicated its duty in that regard. No matter that we were trying to save what was left of a little girl's ravaged psyche and possibly her life.

Lennox was the polar opposite of Gambacurta and was the kind of individual who would make anyone at ease in an interview or just shooting the breeze. He had the unenviable task of putting up with my anger at his colleague for the cheap stunt that he had pulled on me with his ratings seeking rant. I told Lennox to let his buddy know that if I ever saw him I would "kick his ass to Bessemer and back." Whether I could have done so is a moot point because I have yet to meet him. But at the time, I was angry enough to have made good on my promise. My righteous indignation was somewhat mollified by the confrontation, even though it was confrontation by proxy. I don't know whatever happened to Gambacurta, I can only assume that his professional career went the way of most hacks – oblivion.

Roper, even though he avoided prison time, still paid a pretty hefty price for his crimes and sins. He had to apologize to Alisa's mother Brenda before each shift of the Hoover Fire Department. The firemen didn't like his being publicly humiliated any more than he did, but they still had to endure it. I can only hope that some of them finally figured out what scum Roper really was under his veneer of being a good guy trapped by a vindictive former wife. Like most people who discover that a friend or a relative that they really like is somebody totally different from their image of him, too many of the firefighters chose to ignore reality. I can only hope that those men have changed their view over the course of the years since Roper was forced to remove his mask.

The real killer for Roper was paying for, and participating in, the making of a video to be shown for educational purposes. I had a friend, Paul Woods, who was a professional in the making of short movie subjects and documentaries. Paul produced a videotaped interview between me and John Roper named "Daddy's Little Girl." It was about twenty minutes long and was the property of the District Attorney's Office to be used by the Prescott House, a location for the interviewing of children who had been victims of sexual abuse.

Prescott House utilized a multi-disciplinary approach designed to bring investigators, prosecutors, child welfare workers and often doctors under the same roof at the same time in order to minimize the trauma that a child victim would experience by being pulled from agency to agency and made to repeat time and again their recollections of the abuse they had suffered. The approach was instituted by the National Child Advocacy Center in Huntsville, Alabama which was the product of former Madison County District Attorney Bud Kramer who had the vision and the initiative to put it all together. Kramer went on several years later to run for and be elected to Congress from his district. The model that he created and refined was soon adopted by various district attorneys across the state and around the country.

David Barber, the District Attorney of Jefferson County adopted the model and a place for children to be interviewed and treated and counseled by trained professionals. It was called the Prescott House, named for the individual who was instrumental in donating time, money and expertise in securing the property. David showed the video on numerous occasions to civic groups, church groups, neighborhood associations and the like to educate the citizenry about child sexual abuse. Aside from educating the general populace about child abuse, showing the video had at least one unexpectedly delicious result. Some lady who attended one of the screenings recognized Roper as the man she had hired to put new carpeting in her house. She went home immediately after watching the video and fired Roper on the spot.

Doug Jones, Roper's attorney, and later my boss when Clinton became womanizer-in-chief, came whining to me that poor John couldn't get work because of the video. It took me several minutes to control my laughter. I can only hope that Roper continued to meet a miserable future every time that he thought that people might have forgotten him. If that sounds harsh and vindictive, so be it. Just remember what he did to Alisa.

And for those of you who are wondering about the possibility that Alisa may have had her secret revealed because of the video, all I can say is that her secret remained one as she had wished. I have stayed in touch with her periodically over the course of the years that have passed since the investigation and prosecution. I speak with her occasionally and received her permission to write about her in this book.

On the plus side, Alisa doesn't feel the shame that almost drove her to taking her own life before she was twelve years old. She has no problem now with my telling her story and is happy that her father was, and is, being exposed for the rapist that he is. Also, she married and worked for a number of years with abused children. Brenda, her mother, had remarried after her divorce from Roper, to Ron, a terrific fellow who became a real and loving dad to both Alisa and John, Jr. And after Roper was exposed for what he did for years to Alisa, Ron adopted both children.

But the ledger also has a debit column which must be acknowledged. Alisa still has many scars, both psychological and physical from what John Roper did to her. The psychological scars haunt her on a regular basis, although she has learned to cope with them. Physically, she suffered terrible internal damage and will never be able to conceive children of her own that she can love with her husband. But she is a survivor and a wonderful person.

As for John Roper, who knows? And who cares? He is not worth thinking about. Lest any of you readers, however, believe that I have lost my anger and vindictiveness over the years, rest assured that in this instance, and a few others, I most assuredly have not. John Roper, wherever you are, may you burn in hell for all eternity. Other than that, have a miserable life.

ALLISON

THE SECOND SURVIVOR I will tell you about also happens to have become one of my best friends. I first heard her voice on the telephone at the district attorney's Office. She identified herself by an assumed name and inquired whether it would be legally possible to prosecute someone who had raped a "friend" of hers years before her inquiry. It was obvious that she was calling about herself and not on behalf of some friend. I persuaded her to meet with me at the Prescott House the next day and she agreed to the meeting.

We had that meeting and I found her to be intelligent, gregarious, candid and very attractive. She was also young, only twenty-three years of age. And after listening to her detail what had occurred to her when she was only seven years of age, I found her story to possess all the earmarks of credibility that every good trial attorney looks for in a potential witness. She was able to provide both significant and seemingly insignificant pieces of corroboration to the allegations of rape. She did so in a fashion that was direct and concise with just a touch of emotion. And she had that indefinable presence, for lack of a better word, that just made a listener want to believe her. A good prosecutor must be skeptical however, and must treat even the most believable witness as potentially exaggerating or even lying about serious allegations.

By the time that we finished a background investigation of both Allison and Leon Albert Prince, the alleged rapist, there was no doubt in the minds of our investigators or in my own mind that Mr. Prince was guilty as hell of raping Allison and of having committed many more crimes against many more children. The problem with Allison's case was the fact that she did not come forward until long after the apparent expiration of the statute of limitations. The statute for the crime of rape was then a mere three years after the crime had been committed. As to why she had chosen this point in her life to come forward, the answer was simple: she had heard that Leon was trying to work with children once again. And Allison Black was not about to let that happen.

Prince's rape of Allison happened some sixteen years prior to my conversation with her. My initial reaction was that somebody needed to shoot this guy because it appeared that we were SOL as far as prosecuting him because the statute had run years before her coming forward. But the more that I thought about this seemingly insurmountable problem, the more I was determined to overcome it. And so I began to act like a lawyer and remembered that the Code of Alabama had been recompiled in 1975, and that a more modern criminal code was substituted for the old one.

A few more gears and wheels began clicking in my head and I remembered some research that Paul Green, now a United States Magistrate Judge, had done when he had worked in the District Attorneys Office. Under the old code, which was in effect at the time that Allison was raped, carnal knowledge (rape) of a female child under the age of twelve was a capital offense with no statute of limitations. Even though the death penalty had been struck down by the Supreme Court in most instances, the offense itself was still governed by the statute in effect at the time of the crime. Thus, the major legal hurdle had been removed, and now, all we had to do was to build a case, indict Prince and then convict the bastard. Simple! Right? Wrong!

Putting together any criminal prosecution is challenging. The prosecutor must learn the facts of the case and determine which ones are both relevant and admissible. He must be familiar enough with the rules of evidence to know where the snags in the river are located. He must have a plan and an alternate plan for negotiating his way through or around these snags. He must be able to simplify his case as much as possible so that it flows smoothly and coherently when presented to a jury. He must be able to anticipate objections from the defense and be able to counter them with legal responses. And he must be able to anticipate possible defenses offered by the defendant's mouthpiece, excuse me, attorney. And all of that is just for starters.

And thus began the effort to bring Leon Albert Prince to the bar of justice, as well as to stop him dead in his tracks from raping, sodomizing and otherwise molesting other young girls and boys. Our investigation confirmed to us that he hadn't even slowed down over the years. In fact, once Leon actually went to trial – which was highly publicized – the cards and letters from young adult men and women who Leon had defiled when they were much younger came pouring into the office. But, I'm getting ahead of myself.

Allison proved to be a font of information. Memories which could be corroborated in a variety of ways were vivid and compelling. Her memory was phenomenal, particularly with an eye for detail about Prince's house, where he raped her. Mr. Prince was the trusted youth music director at the church Allison and her family attended in Tarrant City within greater Birmingham.

His position within the congregation put him in perfect position to engage in his avocation of molesting children. And he took full advantage of his proximity with them. The adult members of the congregation trusted him absolutely with a naiveté born of their unquestioning belief in the inherent goodness of man. My years as a prosecutor made me somewhat of a cynic who too often came to the opposite conclusion: "People are no damned good."

During the course of the lengthy investigation which preceded Prince's indictment, other individuals began telling us about Prince's notoriety in Tarrant when they were growing up. It almost seemed as if the adult population in Prince's congregation and neighborhood just stuck there heads in the sand when they should have been sticking Leon Albert Prince in the dirt somewhere in about a six-foot-deep hole. After Prince was indicted, even more people came forward with incidents from their childhood wherein Prince molested them or other people who simply knew him by reputation.

I invested a great deal of time investigating reports of Prince molesting, or attempting to molest young boys and girls. One very disturbing occurrence involving Prince and a young teenage girl from Texas posed many questions, none of which were ever resolved, but I knew that the full story would never be told. It seems that Leon had moved to Austin, Texas sometime in the 1970's or '80's for whatever purpose. He began squiring a young girl of about the age of fifteen. Yes, Mr. Prince occasionally took out "older" women such as this ingénue. One night, Leon apparently was out with another person, at least someone who provided him with a plausible alibi. When he returned home, the young fifteen-year-old was found dead in his carport, hanging by a rope attached to her neck and a cross beam. I guess that it was just another coincidental tragedy involving Mr. Prince.

And of course, the story wouldn't be complete without mentioning Angela, Prince's daughter, who was subjected to his evil "amusements" for much of her life, a life that should have been that of a lovely and normal young lady, but which became that of a drug addicted husk of a person by the time that she was little older than a teen-ager. I met Angela during the course of doing the background investigation on Leon. Allison had a strong memory of Leon molesting a young girl about the age of two or three when he was raping and molesting Allison who was then about seven years of age. He molested this child while Allison, too terrified to move, watched Prince rape a young child on the living room floor. Knowing that he had a daughter who was about the same age as the young child would have been, made our investigation of Prince even more intense.

Paul Skaggs, an officer with the Trussville Police Department was assisting me with the investigation of Prince because that suburb of Birmingham was now Leon's city of residence. The Truss-ville, P.D. was familiar with Angela and her husband, a total bum who made his living on the wrong side of the law. Angela, by then a drug-addicted young woman barely twenty years old, had a bad habit of writing checks with insufficient funds to cover them.

Skaggs called me one day and told me that he had persuaded Angela to come into his office for the purpose of working out a payment schedule on some of the checks. This opportunity was perfect for questioning Angela as to whether she too had been one of Leon's victims. And we came up with a plan that was designed to get information without really telling Angela, so as not to taint her responses. Skaggs introduced me to her, and I was very casual in my telling her that if she made restitution on the bad checks, she could be put on probation and her record would be expunged. However, if she failed to make good on the checks and/or got into any further trouble she would be put in jail on the old charges for six months, as well as doing more time on any new charges.

She had no idea why she was actually talking with me, and I told her that I would need some biographical information on her family in order to determine whether there were any outstanding warrants on any of them. This request was merely a ploy to relax Angela and to avoid telling the young woman what it was we really wanted to know. We also were surreptitiously taping the entire conversation.

At an appropriate moment in the conversation, I said to Angela, "Why don't you tell us about your father?" She froze and got a look in her eyes like a scared rabbit. At that moment, I locked eyes with her and said "Angela, we know everything!" I hoped that by saying that, it would help to unlock some dreaded memories of her childhood. I couldn't have been more surprised when she burst into tears and poured out a recounting of how Leon had attempted to rape her just three weeks prior to the interview in her own house.

Before it became a completed rape, it was stopped by Angela's husband, a real scum bag in his own right. He should have killed Leon on the spot, instead of merely restraining him. Killing a person in order to prevent rape in the first degree is justifiable homicide in Alabama. But instead of doing the right thing and choking the life right out of the evil monster, Angela's husband decided that there was a buck to be made here. And thus for the price of several pair of new shoes and some dresses for Angela, along with a little cash for himself, Angela's husband proved himself to be the second coming of Judas Iscariot, with Angela's promise to not prosecute. She was so afraid of Leon that she said that she would lie if we attemped to make a criminal case against Leon.

After Angela recounted this incident to us, I questioned her about her childhood, figuring that it would be a recounting of numerous instances of abuse, rape and sodomy. Once again she surprised me, mentioning only a single incident that occurred in a motel room when she was about eleven or twelve years old. I asked her whether Leon had molested her on other occasions when she was a child. Her response was that she couldn't remember anything prior to about the time that she was twelve. I assumed that she meant she couldn't recall any incidents of sexual abuse, but further questioning resulted in her total lack of memory for anything, including names of friends, schools attended, names of teachers, nothing. Draw your own conclusions.

Following this session with Angela, it was apparent that Leon had totally ruined her as a human being, and certainly as a witness. Oh, and did I mention that Angela was pregnant when Leon attempted to rape her? When the baby was born, Leon's former wife who was Angela's mother, adopted the child. Denise and her second husband Don were excellent parents both to Brian, the son of Denise and Leon, as well as to Angela's baby.

The story gets very complicated and difficult to follow at this point. After about a year of investigation and preparation I left the District Attorney's Office and went to work for the United States Attorney. I had postponed my departure for several months until the United States Attorney told me that he had to fill the position in the near future or the Justice Department would revoke the addition of the newly created position. Faced with that choice, I reluctantly followed through with severing my ties to the District Attorney's Office and moved several blocks down the street to begin my work as a fed.

My last act prior to my departure was to hand off the investigation and place it in the capable hands of Teresa Pulliam. Needless to say, Teresa took the ball and ran with it. The grand jury returned an indictment on two different occasions in this case, the second time being required because the trial judge incorrectly had thrown out the first. The State appealed his ruling and the Court of Criminal Appeals ruled that he should not have dismissed the case. The case went to trial, and Allison was the most compelling witness that I have ever seen. Teresa was absolutely brilliant in her presentation of the evidence. The jury had no trouble convicting Leon in short order, and recommended a sentence of thirty years, a recommendation followed by the judge.

The aftermath is still being played out. Leon served the maximum amount of time for his sentence, which unfortunately under the sentencing provisions in Alabama at the time of his offense, mandated his parole after he had served only slightly more than half his sentence. He was paroled in November of 2007. Allison publicly predicted that within six months of his release, he would be attempting, in some capacity, to work with children. She was far too generous in giving Leon credit for possibly staying away from children for an entire half year. It took him less than three months.

I received a telephone call one evening from Allison, now a successful and poised business woman in her forties. To say that she was hysterical and beside herself significantly understates the emotional breakdown that she was experiencing. I did my dead level best to calm her down and make some semblance of what she was saying. Ultimately, I was able to glean from her, despite her sobs, that Leon Albert Prince, paroled less than six months before Allison's cry in the night to me, already had managed to insert himself into a position similar to that of the fox in the chicken coop.

He had "found the Lord" as so many of these creeps do, but only after they have heard the slamming of the prison gates. And I say that in deference and with great respect to all real Christians, including those criminals who have truly been redeemed. It's simply that far too many Christians are gullible and naïve enough to swallow anything as long as the purveyor of whatever garbage is being sold invokes the name of the Lord. Christians should be more like Ronald Reagan: "Trust, but verify," and less like the people who made millions for P.T. Barnum: "There's a sucker born every minute." But one of the harsh truisms of life is that there never will be a shortage of people more than eager to believe that the wolf in sheep's clothing actually is just a misunderstood wolf who really wants to be a gentle lamb ready to rejoin the flock and not eat the rest of the sheep.

And so it went that Leon Prince, soon after being paroled for raping a seven year old little girl, joined one of the largest congregations in Montgomery and volunteered to help them with their prison ministry. Worse yet, he volunteered to teach the younger inmates who had been incarcerated for various sexual offenses all about the errors of his ways so as to help them better cope with their temptations upon their release. (I couldn't make this stuff up, even if I tried!) And thus, the reason for Allison's hysterical telephone call to me at home.

Upon learning of this not unexpected development, the two of us launched a series of calls to the congregation's pastor, the newspapers, television news outlets and the State Attorney General's Office. In addition to Leon's volunteer work with the church in the prison ministry, some well intentioned idiot had determined that Prince wasn't covered by Meagan's Law. This statute required the State to maintain a registry of locations for sex offenders who were not in prison.

Ironically, Allison had worked night and day in her lobbying efforts, ensuring that all fifty states adopt that law. Once it became known to the general public that this child rapist could possibly move into the house next door and not be subjected to the notification requirement imposed by Meagan's Law, reaction was both swift and positive. The courts held that simply because Meagan's Law was not in existence when Prince raped Allison, the notification and registry requirements of that statute did not constitute an *ex post facto* law, and Prince was subject to its requirements. And Mr. Prince also was relieved of his duties as a "mentor" to young inmates serving time for sexual offenses.

Allison Black Cornelius, I am proud to say, has gone on to achieve regional and national recognition as an advocate for children. She also has her own business, directed at teaching non-profit organizations and aspiring board members of such organizations the best ways of achieving their goals. She has been admitted as a student at various mini-courses at universities around the country and has also taught at educational institutions such as Harvard. To say that she has been successful in her field of expertise is akin to saying that a George Patton was a pretty good general.

Allison is my friend and exemplifies the reasons that made me love my work. I am grateful for every day that I was a prosecutor and for the opportunities I was given to make a difference in the lives of a few individuals along the way. I have regrets for more than a few transgressions and omissions in my life, but I thank God for the time that I was given to make a difference.

AFTERWORD

AND SO IT WENT during the time that I represented the citizens of Alabama. As I have written, after eight and a half years as a state prosecutor, I became a federal prosecutor for the next fourteen and a half years. Not a day goes by that I don't miss the job, nor does a day go by that I miss the bureaucracy. I learned the hard way that there is always something bitter-sweet about any job. But I did discover that if you are fortunate and the gods smile upon you, you can find that niche in life that has your name on it. I found my niche, and I milked it for every bit of gratification and satisfaction that I could squeeze from it.

Probably the closest I can come to adequately describing my feelings about my profession is to paraphrase a brief soliloquy from the movie *Fractured*: The advice is rendered by a wise judge to a young prosecutor trying to decide whether to remain a prosecutor or to accept a job as a litigator with a prestigious civil law firm.

"There's something to be said for those low paying civil service jobs. Oh, they won't get you into the right country club, and your golfing buddies in the men's locker room won't be talking about you and your partners in the firm, but every so often you will have the opportunity to drive a

stake right through the bad guy's heart. And you can't put a price on that experience."

To justice and those who fight for it.

Bob McGregor,

A Prosecutor

www.ingramcontent.com/pod-product-compliance
Lightning Source LLC
Chambersburg PA
CBHW030303290526
45785CB00001B/190